Studies in the
Book of Revelation

Mike Bickle

Studies in the Book of Revelation by Mike Bickle

Published by Forerunner Publishing
International House of Prayer
3535 E. Red Bridge Road
Kansas City, MO 64137

ihopkc.org/books
mikebickle.org

Forerunner Publishing is the book-publishing division of the International House of Prayer of Kansas City, an evangelical missions organization that exists to partner in the Great Commission by advancing 24/7 prayer and proclaiming the beauty of Jesus and His glorious return.

ISBN: 978-1-938060-48-9

Cover design by IHOPKC Marketing
Printed in the United States of America

Studies in the Book of Revelation
Mike Bickle

CONTENTS

Electronic copies of these notes are available at mikebickle.org
DVDs of this teaching series are available at store.ihopkc.org

Session 1: Introduction and Overview of the Book of Revelation

The Unveiling of the Man Jesus.

I. THE BOOK OF REVELATION: JESUS' END-TIME BATTLE PLAN FOR THE CHURCH

A. The book of Revelation reveals the glory of Jesus (Rev. 1:1) and His plan to transition the earth to the age to come. The book is called *The Revelation of Jesus* because it reveals His heart, power, and leadership in preparing the nations for God's glory. One of the Father's purposes in giving this book to the Church is to reveal the beauty of Jesus. It is secondarily a book about "events" in the end times. The main theme is not God's plan, but the glory of the Man behind the plan.

> [1]*The Revelation of Jesus Christ, which God gave Him to show His servants—things which must shortly take place. And He sent and signified it by His angel to His servant John. (Rev. 1:1)*

B. The main theme in God's plan in the book of Revelation is Jesus' return to earth as king to rule all the nations (Rev. 1:7). His "royal procession" back to earth will be seen by every person.

> [7]*Behold, He is coming with clouds, and every eye will see Him. (Rev. 1:7)*

C. If we read Revelation correctly, it causes us to love Jesus and trust His leadership, as we see His dramatic plans for the end times. His wise and loving plans combine God's sovereignty (in manifesting love and righteousness), human free will, and satanic rage resulting in the end-time harvest of souls and a victorious Church, without violating justice or man's free will. The Lord's plan is for an environment that allows both love and wickedness to come to full expression.

An example to follow

D. The Bereans searched the Scriptures to see if the things that Paul said were true (Acts 17:10–11). I do not ask anyone to accept my views; rather, I urge you to think for yourself. Truth is never hurt by scrutiny, but rather it is confirmed. You must boldly challenge all ideas that you hear. I urge you to refuse any teaching that you do not clearly see with your eyes in your Bible. ✳

> [11]*These were more fair-minded…in that they received the word with all readiness, and searched the Scriptures daily to find out whether these things were so. (Acts 17:11)*

we must only speak truth!

E. When speaking about Scripture, people may speak from one of three positions. It is important to make clear which position we are speaking from. We are to boldly proclaim *biblical convictions*, carefully qualify our *informed opinions*, and rarely speak about our *personal theories*. ✳

Andrew; WARNING.

F. The most controversial point in this study is found in my belief that the Church will go through the Tribulation (in great victory and power). This differs from the popular pretribulation rapture view that teaches that the Church will be raptured at any minute and miss the end-time revival and crisis. Yes, the Bible teaches that the Church will be raptured. The issue is one of timing.

G. I believe that the Church will be raptured at the end of the tribulation, not the beginning. I greatly honor the godliness and wisdom of many who hold the pretribulation rapture view, but I see it as a mistake that will leave many spiritually unprepared. We can disagree in a spirit of meekness, without a spirit of debate. The reality of the Tribulation is too weighty to reduce it to arguments.

H. Revelation gives us more information on the end times than any other book in Scripture. It was written to help God's people participate in the end-time drama that shifts history to the age to come and endure persecution and temptation so as to overcome in victory (Rev. 12:11; 15:2).

I. Revelation is the only book of the Bible in which God promises a special blessing to anyone who reads or hears it (Rev. 1:3), but issues a grave warning to any who add to or take from it (Rev. 22:18–19).

> ^{3}*Blessed is he who* <u>*reads*</u> *and those who* <u>*hear*</u> *the words of this prophecy. (Rev. 1:3)*

J. Revelation was written to be understood by God's people, even the poor and uneducated. A common lie must be exposed—that this book cannot be understood except by scholars.

K. *Unique dynamics* will exist in the generation in which Jesus returns, including the greatest measure of unity, purity, and power in the Church, in contrast to the greatest measure of sin and oppression in the nations, which will be confronted by the greatest measure of God's judgment to remove all that hinders love. Jesus desires deep partnership with the Body of Christ in His work.

L. Jesus will judge wickedness and oppression to remove all that hinders love (Rev. 19:2). The Antichrist and the kings of the earth will declare war against Jesus (Rev. 17:14; 19:19; cf. Ps. 2:2). Jesus will war against them (Rev. 19:11). This will be the most violent time in history.

> ^{11}*In righteousness He [Jesus] judges and* <u>*makes war*</u>*…*^{15}*…He should strike the nations…*
> ^{19}*I saw the beast [Antichrist], the kings of the earth, and their armies, gathered together to* <u>*make war against Him*</u> *who sat on the horse and against His army. (Rev. 19:11–19)*

M. Jesus' judgments in the Great Tribulation do not happen *to* God's people as helpless victims of Satan, but they are released *through* them as they partner with His sovereign leadership.

N. As the book of Acts describes the power of the Spirit released through the early church, so the book of Revelation describes the power of the Spirit to be released through the end-time church. I refer to Revelation as the *"end-time book of Acts"* and a *"canonized prayer manual"* that informs the Church of various ways in which Jesus will manifest His power in relationship to the prayers of the whole Body of Christ during the Great Tribulation (Rev. 8:1–6).

O. As Moses participated in prayer under the Lord's leadership in releasing His judgments on Pharaoh (Ex. 7–12), so the end-time Church will participate in prayer under Jesus' leadership as He releases the Great Tribulation judgments on the Antichrist (Rev. 6–19).

P. The type of miracles and judgments seen in the books of Exodus and Acts will be multiplied and released worldwide through prayer in the Tribulation. The greatest demonstrations of power in history will be released by the praying Church operating in unity under Jesus' leadership.

> ^{18}*"I will build My church, and the* <u>*gates of Hades*</u> *[authority of hell]* <u>*shall not prevail against it*</u>*.* ^{19}*And I will give you the* <u>*keys*</u> *of the kingdom of heaven, and* <u>*whatever you bind on earth*</u> *will be bound in heaven, and* <u>*whatever you loose on earth*</u> *will be loosed in heaven."* *(Mt. 16:18–19)*

[12]*"The works that I do he will do also; and <u>greater works than these he will do</u>." (Jn. 14:12)*

II.   THE SYMBOLS IN THE BOOK OF REVELATION

A.   There are seven main symbols in the book of Revelation. The events and numbers in Revelation are to be taken in their plain meaning (literal) unless the passage clearly indicates that they are symbolic (Rev. 1:20; 5:6; 11:8; 12:1, 3, 9; 17:7, 9, 15–18, etc.).

B.   ***Dragon***: symbolic of Satan (Rev. 12:3, 4, 7, 9, 13, 16, 17; 13:2, 4; 16:13; 20:2)

C.   ***First beast***: symbolic of the Antichrist (Rev. 13; 14:9–11; 17:3–17; 19:19–21; 20:4, 10)

D.   ***Another beast***: symbolic of the False Prophet, called "another beast" just once (Rev. 13:11)

E.   ***Seven heads***: seven empires from history that persecuted Israel (Egypt, Assyria, Babylon, Persia, Greece, Rome, revived Roman Empire of Dan. 2:41–42; 7:7; Rev. 12:3; 13:1; 17:3–16)

F.   ***Ten horns***: represent a ten-nation confederation that serves the Antichrist (Rev. 17:12–13)

G.   ***Harlot Babylon***: points to a demonically inspired religious and economic system (Rev. 17–18)

H.   ***Woman with a male-child*** *(Jesus)*: the faithful remnant of Israel through history (Rev. 12)

III.   STRUCTURE OF REVELATION: 4 PARTS

A.   There are *4 parts* in the structure of the book of Revelation, the fourth part being the largest and consisting of *5 chronological sections* in which the events occur in sequential order.

B.   ***Part 1: John's <u>calling</u> to prophesy about the end times (Rev. 1)***. John gave truths about Jesus' majesty that formed the way he prophesied about the end times. These truths are also to equip us.

C.   ***Part 2: Jesus gave <u>7 letters</u> to the churches (Rev. 2–3)***. The instructions Jesus gave to these churches about overcoming sin give insight into what the end-time church must overcome.

D.   ***Part 3: Jesus takes <u>the scroll</u> (Rev. 4–5)***. This contains the earth's title deed and Jesus' plan to cleanse the earth. Jesus takes a 7-sealed scroll from the Father, representing the ***title deed*** of the earth and the ***battle plan*** to judge, cleanse, and prepare the nations for Jesus' rule over the earth, while bringing the Church to maturity, a Bride to partner with Him in His plan (Rev. 6–22).

E.   ***Part 4: Jesus' <u>battle plan</u> (Rev. 6–22)***. This includes the Great Tribulation judgments against the Antichrist. Jesus reveals His main storyline of love to cleanse the earth of evil. His battle plan is seen in ***5 chronological sections*** describing the main storyline of the 21 judgment events (7 seals, 7 trumpets, and 7 bowls) that are released on the Antichrist's empire in sequential order.

F.   After each chronological section, an angel explains to John why the events just described are necessary. The angelic explanations function as parentheses that put the storyline on "pause." They answer questions arising from the chronological sections: Why is God's wrath so severe? What will happen to the saints? Angels explain to John *what happens to God's people*, including what Jesus will do to *help them* and what the Antichrist will do to *persecute them*.

IV.   FIVE CHRONOLOGICAL SECTIONS (REV. 6–22)

A.   *Chronological Section #1 (Rev. 6)*. The seal judgments against the kingdom of darkness. Angelic Explanation #1 (Rev. 7). We receive *protection* from judgments and falling away.

B.   *Chronological Section #2 (Rev. 8–9)*. The *trumpet judgments* against the Antichrist's empire. Angelic Explanation #2 (Rev. 10–11). We receive *direction* by increased prophetic ministry.

C.   *Chronological Section #3 (Rev. 11:15–19)*. Jesus' *second coming royal procession* and the rapture leading to Jesus replacing all the kings and top governmental leaders on earth. Angelic Explanation #3 (Rev. 12–14). The Antichrist's violent *confrontation* with the saints deserves Jesus' judgment and the replacement of all his evil governments.

1.   At the 7th and last trumpet (1 Thes. 4:16; 1 Cor. 15:52; Rev. 10:7), Jesus will rapture the Church and travel across the sky in a royal procession, so that every eye will see Him (Rev. 1:7).

> [7] *Behold, He is coming with clouds, and <u>every eye will see Him</u>, even they who pierced Him. And all the tribes of the earth will <u>mourn</u> because of Him. (Rev. 1:7)*

2.   After this, Jesus will enter Jerusalem and stand on the Mount of Olives (Zech. 14:4).

D.   *Chronological Section #4 (Rev. 15–16)*. *Bowl judgments* destroy evil infrastructures in society. Angelic Explanation #4 (Rev. 17–18). The *seduction* of Babylon's evil religion will permeate and infiltrate all the structures of society, requiring that Babylon be totally destroyed.

E.   *Chronological Section #5 (Rev. 19–20)*. Jesus' *triumphal entry* into Jerusalem (Rev. 19:11–21:8). Angelic Explanation #5 (Rev. 21–22). The *restoration* of all things, Acts 3:21 (Rev. 21:9–22:5).

> [15] *Now out of His mouth goes a sharp sword, that with it He should strike the nations. And He Himself will rule them…* [16] *And He has on His robe and on His thigh a name written: KING OF KINGS AND LORD OF LORDS…* [19] *And I saw the beast, the kings of the earth, and their armies, gathered together to make war against Him…* [20] *Then the beast was captured, and with him the false prophet…These two were cast alive into the lake of fire…* [21] *The rest were killed with the sword…* [20:1] *Then I saw an angel coming down from heaven, having the key to the bottomless pit and a great chain in his hand.* [2] *He laid hold of…Satan, and bound him for a thousand years;* [3] *…so that he should deceive the nations no more till the thousand years were finished…* [4] *And I saw thrones, and they sat on them, and judgment was committed to them… And they lived and reigned with Christ for a thousand years. (Rev. 19:15–20:4)*

Session 2: The Varying Importance of End-Time Beliefs

I.   INTRODUCTION

A.   This is a working document that we will add to from time to time.

B.   We recognize varying degrees of importance regarding biblical, end-time beliefs and themes. We use four categories of ideas related to the end times—those of *primary importance* (essential doctrines), those held as our *core convictions*, those *helpful for clarity*, and personal *opinions*.

C.   Jesus spoke of some truths as being weightier than others (Mt. 23:23), and He considered the commandment to love God to be "greater" than other commandments (Mt. 22:37–38).

²³ "You tithe mint and dill and cummin, and have neglected the <u>weightier provisions</u> of the law: justice and mercy and faithfulness." (Mt. 23:23 NASB)

D.   It is important to present the biblical message of the end times with humility and in a way that promotes unity, yet without compromising important truths. This is captured in the well-known saying *"In essentials, unity; in non-essentials, liberty; in all things, love."*

E.   The Lord wants His people to be bold, with strong convictions about what the Bible makes clear, yet with humility and proper nuance. We acknowledge the value of people whose views differ from our own, and we must always posture ourselves to continue to learn and listen to others.

F.   In our zeal to be faithful to the Scriptures, we acknowledge that some end-time themes are best stated as opinions and suggestions, instead of as statements that are unnecessarily dogmatic. Scripture allows for interpretative diversity concerning the specific details and timing of events.

G.   Any presentation of a detailed narrative of future events from a biblical perspective must be tempered, knowing that church history is littered with self-confident teachers who proudly overstated their position or were dogmatic where the Scriptures were not. It is best to delineate between primary truths and our personal opinions when presenting details of end-time themes.

H.   No group has more than part of the full truth of Scripture about the end times. Only as the *whole Body of Christ receives understanding* will we know the full biblical storyline.

I.   We are to respect others with differing views on the end times, as long as biblical eschatological essentials are upheld and sound, contextual Bible interpretation is implemented. Teachers must be careful not to imply that their view on the end times is the only correct one.

J.   The purpose of this message is to emphasize that there are varying levels of importance of end-time doctrines and themes, and that our staff, students, interns, and other members of this spiritual family do not need to embrace *all* that we say about the end times. I do not ask anyone to accept my views; rather, I urge you to think for yourself (Acts 17:10–11), to boldly challenge all ideas that you hear, and refuse any teaching that you do not see with your eyes in your Bible.

II.   PRIMARY IMPORTANCE: ESSENTIAL DOCTRINES

These are truths that have been upheld historically by the Church as essential doctrines of salvation. They define what is essential orthodoxy as related to end-time themes. The truths below do not include all the important doctrines in our statement of faith, but only those pertaining to the end times. We agree with the Apostles' Creed, the Nicene Creed, and the Athanasian Creed.

A.   **_Authority of Scripture_**: We fully agree with the reformers who used the phrase **_Sola Scriptura._** Our one source for understanding God's plan for the end times is Scripture alone. We do not base our views on prophetic experiences or "personal revelations." The only sure commentary on the Word is the Word itself.

B.   **_Second coming_**: The literal, bodily, second coming of Jesus to reign forever as King of kings

C.   **_Resurrection of the saints_**: The physical or bodily resurrection of the saints

D.   **_Heaven_**: Living with Jesus in the New Jerusalem on the new earth for all eternity

E.   **_Eternal judgment_**: The punishment of the lost. We stand strongly against the heresy of universalism that teaches that there is no hell and that all people will be saved.

III.   CORE CONVICTIONS

A.   Below are core convictions that our leadership holds related to the end times. We do not require our staff, students, interns, or other members of this spiritual family to embrace these truths, yet it is necessary for all who teach at IHOPU to uphold our core convictions. Part of our calling is to be a "messaging ministry," committed to being faithful witnesses of Jesus, His plan of salvation, His commitment to build the Church and disciple nations, and of His end-time plans.

B.   Our leadership team has worked through our core convictions for many years, even decades. We have based them on the Scriptures, with the confirmation of many teachers in the Church.*

C.   Our leadership team has been thoroughly exposed to different views held by others in the Body of Christ. We are aware of these differing views and are firmly settled on our core convictions.

D.   We welcome any to challenge our views as they seek to establish their own core convictions. We value this process for them. We are committed to our core convictions, but remain open to change our views related to biblical end-time themes that are of lesser importance (see page 8).

E.   We seek to be clear about our core convictions, so that people do not join us thinking that they might change them. We love and honor believers who disagree with our core convictions and encourage them to find a spiritual family where they can enjoy unity related to their convictions.

F.   Our primary end-time theology is **historic premillennialism with a victorious church**. After many years of searching the Word and studying the writings of other ministries, our leadership team is firmly convinced that this is the end-time position that is most faithful to what we believe the Scriptures teach. Our core convictions express this theological perspective.

G.   **_Historic premillennialism and the victorious Church_**—this represents our core beliefs related to the end times. Many teachers throughout church history, and today, have held to historic premillennialism and/or a victorious Church.* This theological view includes the following:

    1.   The victorious Church walking in unity, intimacy, and maturity (purity, power, wisdom). Unity includes the whole Church working together in love and honor (Jn. 17:21–23). Jesus loves the whole Church and is returning for a large, unified, international Church.

    ¹³...till we all come to the <u>unity</u> of the faith and of the <u>knowledge</u> of the Son of God [intimacy], to a <u>perfect man</u> [maturity], to...the fullness of Christ. (Eph. 4:13)

    2.   The theme of a victorious church includes a global harvest and a prayer and worship movement from every nation preceding Jesus' return (Mt. 24:14; Rev. 5:9; 7:9, 14).

    3.   The Millennium, a 1,000-year reign of Jesus on the earth with the saints (Rev. 20:1–6). We believe that the Church is to impact society with the kingdom, but we do not embrace the postmillennial view that society will be fully Christianized before Jesus returns.

    4.   The Antichrist is a man who will be the most powerful demonic leader in history

    5.   A post-tribulation rapture at the end of the Great Tribulation, which lasts 3½ years

    6.   A futurist view of most of the prophecies found in the books of Revelation and Daniel

    7.   Global temporal judgments preceding the return of the Lord

    8.   The abomination of desolation is the primary sign that Jesus gave for recognizing the beginning of the Great Tribulation. It includes the image and mark of the beast (Rev. 13).

    9.   A falling away from the faith (Mt. 24:9–13; 2 Thes. 2:3; 1 Tim. 4:1–2; 2 Tim. 3:1–7; 4:3–5; 2 Pet. 2:1–3)

    10.   Eternal rewards and reigning on the earth with Jesus (Rev. 2:26; 3:21; 5:10; 20:4–6; 22:5)

H.   Jesus as Bridegroom, King, and Judge: Jesus is a Bridegroom with desire, a King with power, and a Judge who is zealous to remove all that hinders love.

I.   The salvation of Israel, the battle for Jerusalem, and supporting the messianic remnant now; the persecution of Israel and widespread anti-Semitism, even including prison camps

J.   The eternal, conscious torment of the damned in the lake of fire (Rev. 14:10–11)

K.   In light of our core convictions, we are committed to raising up forerunners who prepare themselves and others spiritually by understanding the unique dynamics seen in the 150 chapters of the Bible whose primary theme is the end times.* Forerunners proclaim Jesus as Bridegroom, King, and Judge and declare what the Scriptures say about the unique dynamics of His end-time plan. They are to equip people so that they are not *offended* by Jesus' leadership, *deceived* by the enemy, *seduced* by the culture, or *fearful of* and *confused* by what will occur in the end times.

IV.   HELPFUL BUT NOT ESSENTIAL

These themes are helpful for those seeking to understand the broader storyline in the Scripture related to the end times. Understanding these themes helps us to grasp many end-time passages that are commonly neglected based on their being difficult to comprehend outside the context of the broader biblical story line. These are not core convictions that we require our teachers, staff, or students to embrace.

A.   Seeing the structure of the book of Revelation as *sequential* (instead of recapitulation) and the three numbered-judgments series (the seals, trumpets, and bowls) as *literal* (instead of symbolic)

B.   The 2-fold definition of the Day of the Lord—the narrow day (24 hours) and the broad day

C.   Identification of the Harlot Babylon

D.   The descent of the New Jerusalem in *proximity* to the earth at the beginning of the Millennium, and *resting on* the earth at the end of the Millennium (Rev. 3:12; 21:2, 10) with regard to the heavenly and earthly realms being joined together at the time of Jesus' return (Eph. 1:10)

E.   Signs of the times: identifying *what* they are and *how* they are fulfilled in today's society

F.   Daniel's 30 days (Rev. 11:2–3; 12:6, 14; 13:5; cf. Dan. 7:25; 12:7, 11)

G.   Jesus marching up from Edom to Jerusalem (Isa. 63), and His royal procession being seen by "every eye" in every part of the earth (Mt. 24:30; Rev. 1:7; cf. Zech. 9:14; 12:10; Mt. 26:64)

V.   OPINIONS THAT ARE NOT CENTRAL

Opinions based on implications drawn from Scripture—these are not central to our core convictions.

A.   My personal **opinion** (not prophecy) that we **may** be in the early days of the generation that the Lord returns is not a conviction held by all in our leadership team. I share this opinion because of my sense of urgency as to the importance of people studying the 150 key end-time chapters.*

B.   The identification and timing of the 144,000 people sealed during the Tribulation

C.   The hastening of the Day of the Lord involves a combination of significant issues, such as the sovereign timing of the Father and the maturity of the Church worldwide (2 Pet. 3:11–14). The end-time global prayer movement is an important part of this, but it is not the only vital issue.

D.   The Church is not to pray for Jesus' return until after the abomination of desolation occurs. We pray, "Come, Lord Jesus!"—come **near us** (in intimacy), **to us** (in revival and justice), and **for us** (at the second coming). The *whole Body of Christ* will be involved in "singing back" the King.

*For additional study material pertaining to this session, see mikebickle.org

Session 3: The Theme of the Book of Revelation (Rev. 1)

I.   INTRODUCTION (REV. 1:1–2)

A.   The book of Revelation is called the *revelation of Jesus* because first it reveals the majesty of His heart and leadership in His plan to transition history to the age to come.

> [1] *The <u>Revelation of Jesus Christ</u>, which God gave Him [Jesus] to show His servants—<u>things</u> which must shortly take place. And He sent and <u>signified it by His angel</u> to…John. (Rev. 1:1)*

B.   Second, it is a book about events that take place in His end-time plan to purify the Church, bring in the harvest, and replace all the evil governments on earth. God's purpose in this book is first to *reveal the Man* behind the plan. Many only see the plan and miss the Man.

C.   In Revelation 1–3, John reports a visionary experience which highlights **30 specific descriptions** of Jesus' majesty, ministry, and personality along with 18 eternal rewards.

   1.   We can identify these 30 descriptions from Jesus' titles, names, appearance, actions, and clothing. For example, the garments that He wore speak of Him as a high priest. His eyes like fire reveal His passion, intensity, judgment, and full knowledge of every situation.

   2.   There are 24 descriptions in Revelation 1 plus 18 in Revelation 2–3, totaling 42. Since 12 are used in both Revelation 1 and Revelation 2–3, there are 30 distinct descriptions.

D.   John gave only abbreviated statements of each description and reward. Each phrase is significant and is but a *hint* that we are to search out more by using the rest of the Bible to get a greater picture of what the Spirit is saying about Jesus. It is like a *menu* highlighting what the Holy Spirit will feed the Church to equip her to overcome temptation and persecution.

E.   Each description and reward communicates a specific insight about Jesus that is necessary in equipping the Church to overcome compromise, endure persecution, and engage in partnership with Jesus in the great end-time drama.

F.   Revelation 1 is the most complete picture of Jesus in the Bible. It describes **who He is** (how He thinks and feels) and **what He does** in His end-time plan. If we read Revelation with the right perspective, it inspires us to adore Jesus and trust His leadership. Here we see what Jesus wants emphasized most about Himself to prepare His Church for the greatest release of His glory.

G.   Jesus gave us these insights into His heart and ministry to form the way we pray, prophesy, and serve Him in releasing His glory and warring against evil. With these insights, we will prophesy with a spirit of boldness, tenderness, and confidence, instead of harshness and fear.

H.   No aspect of God's grace more powerfully transforms our emotions or satisfies us than when God the Spirit reveals God to our hearts. *Is your life goal to enter into the power and pleasure of being obsessed with Jesus' magnificence?* I want to be obsessed with His magnificence.

I.   Insight into Jesus equips us to *overcome temptation*, to *endure persecution*, and to *engage in partnership* with His end-time plan to transition the earth to the age to come.

J.   Paul gladly gave up everything as he saw the magnificence, or excellence, of Jesus! If we can see what Paul saw about Jesus, then we can live like he lived. Paul would have given up anything to position his heart to gain more insight into Jesus' magnificence and to feel the power of it.

[8]I also count all things loss for the <u>excellence</u> [magnificence] of the knowledge of Christ Jesus… (Phil. 3:8)

K.   The Spirit was given to us to be our escort into the deep things of God's heart. He knows more about Jesus than we can imagine. He will reveal as much of Jesus as we are hungry for. He gives to us based on our hunger for more. He will not force-feed us. I pray, "Holy Spirit, let me see what You see and feel what You feel about Jesus—teach me about Him."

[13]"The Spirit…will <u>guide</u> [escort] you…[14]He will take of what is Mine and <u>declare it to you</u>." (Jn. 16:13–14)

[10]The Spirit searches…the <u>deep things of God</u>…[12]We have received…the Spirit who is from God, <u>that we might know</u> the things that have been freely given to us by God. (1 Cor. 2:10–12)

L.   The Spirit is raising up those who will proclaim the riches of Jesus. The most neglected subject in the kingdom of God is God Himself. We must not only teach on topics such as leadership and relationship skills, economic principles, ministry skills, how to be happier, etc.

[8]To me…grace was given, that I should preach…the <u>unsearchable riches</u> of Christ. (Eph. 3:8)

M.   In Revelation 1, Jesus is seen as the *Son of Man* who leads the Church through history as the *Prophet, Priest, and King*. These truths are to equip the church (Rev. 2–3) to be faithful to Him.

[13]…One like the <u>Son of Man</u>, clothed with a <u>garment</u> down to the feet…(Rev. 1:13)

1.   Jesus used the title *Son of Man* more than any other when speaking of Himself (85 references). When Jesus spoke of Himself as the Son of Man, He proclaimed the two most important truths about Himself, that He was both fully God and fully human. By using this title, Jesus was saying, "I am fully God yet fully human. I am one of you."

2.   As the *Son of Man*, He stood before the throne of God to be commissioned by the Father (Ancient of Days) to rule all the nations on earth (Dan. 7:13–14).

[13]"Behold, One like the <u>Son of Man</u>, coming with the clouds of heaven!…[14]Then to Him was given dominion…His dominion is an everlasting dominion." (Dan. 7:13–14)

N.   In Revelation 1, Jesus' leadership in the Church is seen as the ***<u>righteous prophet</u>, <u>merciful priest</u>***, and ***<u>sovereign king</u>***. However, as the book unfolds, His leadership is openly revealed before all the nations at the end of the age in Rev. 19–22 as the ***Bridegroom, King, and Judge***.

O.   In Revelation 19–22, the righteous prophet is seen in greater light as the ***<u>zealous judge</u>***, the merciful priest as the ***<u>passionate Bridegroom</u>***, and the ***<u>sovereign king</u>***.

II.   A SUMMARY OF THE THEME OF THE BOOK OF REVELATION

A.   Revelation 1:1–8 is a summary of the book of Revelation (Rev. 1:1).

¹The Revelation of Jesus Christ, which God gave Him to show His servants—things which must shortly take place. And He sent and signified it by His angel to His servant John… (Rev. 1:1)

1.   ***Things:*** Jesus revealed "things" or events to come. These are events the Father selected to emphasize. The Father revealed a small percentage of the events that will occur in the generation that Jesus returns in—the ones that He considered as especially strategic.

2.   ***God gave to Jesus:*** The Father "gave" or mandated that Jesus show His servants these events. Jesus commissioned His angel to show these events to John. Thus, we know that the Father wants the servants of God to be familiar with these events. We are to talk about them and not ignore them. This is itself a mandate to study the book of Revelation.

B.   Scripture promised a blessing for anyone who would read and hear these events (Rev. 1:3). This blessing is within the reach of all. It is one of the most neglected blessings in the church today.

³Blessed is he who reads and those who hear the words of this prophecy… (Rev. 1:3)

C.   This information was given to John to give to the churches (Rev. 1:4). John was commanded twelve times to write this prophecy for the benefit of the Church (Rev. 1:11, 19; 2:1, 8, 12, 18; 3:1, 4, 14; 14:13; 19:9; 21:5). This was to be taught in the churches. It can be understood by all.

⁴John, to the seven churches which are in Asia: Grace to you and peace from Him. (Rev. 1:4)

D.   ***Grace and peace:*** Using the truths in the book of Revelation, God will impart peace to overcome fear and grace to resist compromise. Fear and compromise are two temptations in the book.

III.   THE FATHER COMING TO THE EARTH (REV. 1:4)

A.   A key to living with confidence is to see the Father's involvement and commitment to the earth. The phrase He *"who is, who was,* and *who is to come,"* depicts God's relationship to the earth, though it includes more than God's relationship to earth. The Father is coming to the earth.

⁴…peace from Him who is and who was and who is to come… (Rev. 1:4)

³"The tabernacle of God is with men…He will dwell with them [on the earth]…" (Rev. 21:3)

B.   The Father is committed to the earth. This is our hope. Our life focus and confidence is that the Father is coming to the earth and what we are doing contributes to that in a small yet real way.

C.   ***Who was:*** He was deeply involved with the earth from before its foundations in Genesis 1. He has worked out His plans from the beginning and has been involved all along the way. The Father has been deeply involved in the present tense throughout every hour of human history.

D.   ***Who is:*** The Father is currently involved in human history. It is on course, and it is not aimless. It is on a purposeful trajectory that is moving steadily to fulfill God's ultimate purposes.

IV.   THE HOLY SPIRIT IS BEFORE THE FATHER (REV. 1:4)

A.   The Holy Spirit is described in His great diversity, position of honor, and posture of humility.

> *⁴…peace from Him…and from the seven Spirits who are before His throne… (Rev. 1:4)*

B.   **Seven Spirits:** The one Holy Spirit is described as the seven Spirits to emphasize His great diversity in function and ability (Isa. 11:2; Rev. 3:1; 4:5; 5:6; cf. Zech. 3:9; 4:10).

> *²The Spirit of the LORD shall rest upon Him, the Spirit of wisdom and understanding, the Spirit of counsel and might, the Spirit of knowledge and of the fear of the LORD. (Isa. 11:2)*

C.   **Before the throne:** The Holy Spirit is "before" the throne, speaking of His position of supreme honor and power as God and of His posture of serving the Father's plan with humility.

V.   THREE FOUNDATIONAL TITLES OF JESUS (REV. 1:5)

A.   John highlighted three primary truths about Jesus (v. 5) on which he elaborated (v. 10–20). This description of Jesus is foundational to understanding and responding to God's plan in Revelation.

> *⁵…from Jesus Christ, the <u>faithful witness</u>, the <u>firstborn from the dead</u>, and <u>the ruler over the kings of the earth</u>. (Rev. 1:5)*

B.   **Faithful witness:** Jesus told the truth about God, man, Israel, culture, the end times, etc. Jesus embodied truth in His life and courageously spoke truth out of loyal love to His Father. This is Jesus' first title in the book and is one of the most important challenges for us to imitate.

1.   Jesus was the faithful witness in His earthly ministry (Rev. 1:5; 3:7, 14; 19:11). Jesus revealed the truth and stood for it regardless of the cost. It resulted in His death.

2.   Jesus did not hold back the negative (rebukes or declarations of judgment) or exaggerate the positive (affirmations or promises). He spoke without regard to the criticism or loss.

C.   **Firstborn among the dead:** Jesus is preeminent in authority over the supernatural realm as its human heir. He occupies the first place of authority and honor as the firstborn of creation. This does not mean He was the first one created, but rather that He is the "first" in *cause and authority*. The power over creation "begins" with Him. He is the first man with a resurrected body and is in the position of the firstborn son as the unique heir of God. He is the *firstborn* from the dead and the *firstfruits* of those who have died (1 Cor. 15:23).

> *¹⁵He is…the <u>firstborn over all creation</u>. ¹⁶By Him all things were created…¹⁸He…is the <u>beginning</u>, the <u>firstborn from the dead</u>, that in all things He may have the <u>preeminence</u>. (Col. 1:15–18)*

D.   **Ruler of the kings of the earth:** Jesus is preeminent in authority over the earthly realm of government. The theme of the book of Revelation is that Jesus is returning to earth to rule all the nations as King of all kings (Rev. 1:5, 7; 11:15; 15:3; 19:16; 21:24). In the Millennium, all the kings of the earth will be saved and worship Him (Ps. 72:11; 102:15; 138:4; 148:11; Isa. 62:2).

> *¹¹All kings shall fall down before Him; <u>all nations</u> shall serve Him. (Ps. 72:11)*

VI.   JESUS AS THE ONE WHO LOVED US AND MADE US KINGS AND PRIESTS (REV. 1:5–6)

A.   Jesus uses His position of honor as heir in the realm of the spirit and ruler of the earth to express love to us by qualifying us to draw close to God and exalting us to rule with Him.

⁵To Him who <u>loved</u> us and <u>washed</u> us from our sins in His own blood, ⁶and has made us <u>kings</u> and <u>priests</u> to His God and Father… (Rev. 1:5–6)

B.   We see a three-fold description of His high priestly ministry for us. He loved or desired us to be His Bride. He washed or cleansed and qualified us to relate closely to God as priests. He exalted us by including us as kings in His reign.

C.   Jesus will govern the earth in partnership with resurrected saints (Rev. 2:26–27; 3:21; 5:10; 20:4–6; 22:5; Mt. 19:28; 20:21–23; 25:23; Lk. 19:17–19; 22:29–30; Rom. 8:17; 1 Cor. 6:2–3).

⁴I saw thrones, and they sat on them…and <u>reigned with Christ for 1,000 years</u>…⁶They shall be <u>priests</u> of God and of Christ, and shall <u>reign</u> with Him 1,000 years. (Rev. 20:4–6)

VII.   JESUS IS COMING TO THE EARTH (REV. 1:7–8)

A.   The primary theme and story line in the book of Revelation is Jesus' coming to the earth on the clouds to be received as king. His kingship will be announced and asserted over every nation as His royal procession in the sky is seen by every eye (Mt. 24:30; Rev. 1:7). Jesus will come to the earth to create the context for the Father to come (1:4, 8; 21:3).

⁷Behold, He is coming with clouds, and <u>every eye will see Him</u>, even they who pierced Him. And <u>all the tribes of the earth</u> will mourn because of Him. (Rev. 1:7)

³⁰"…and then <u>all the tribes of the earth</u> will mourn, and <u>they will see</u> the Son of Man coming on the clouds of heaven with power and great glory." (Mt. 24:30)

B.   All the unbelievers in all the nations will see Him. Mourning describes either their repentance unto salvation (Zech. 12:10) or remorse over their coming judgment (Rev. 1:7; 16:9, 11, 21).

VIII.   JESUS AS THE SON OF MAN: LIVING FASCINATED (REV. 1:9–20)

A.   John was not focused on his limitations and tribulations, but was awestruck. The body of Christ is so familiar with "the God that we hardly know" so that we are tempted to stay focused on our lonely "prison island" instead of turning to hear the voice of the Man who alone can fascinate us.

⁹I, John…was on the island that is called <u>Patmos</u> for the word of God…¹²I turned to see the voice that spoke…and having turned I saw…¹³One like the <u>Son of Man</u>… (Rev. 1:9–13)

B.   Jesus revealed His majesty as the Son of Man who is Prophet, Priest, and King (Rev. 1:13–17).

¹⁴His <u>head</u> and <u>hair</u> were white like wool, as white as snow, and His <u>eyes</u> like a flame of fire; ¹⁵His <u>feet</u> were like fine brass, as if refined in a furnace, and His <u>voice</u> as the sound of many waters; ¹⁶…out of His <u>mouth</u> went a sharp two-edged sword, and His <u>countenance</u> was like the sun shining in its strength. ¹⁷And when I saw Him, <u>I fell</u> at His feet as dead. (Rev. 1:14–17)

C.   *Jesus' eyes:* His "eyes like fire" speak of His burning desire of love, His intensity, and His knowledge that penetrate all things as fire penetrates metal. They speak of His ability to *see* everything, to *feel* love for us, to *impart* love to us, and to *destroy* all that hinders love.

¹⁴His <u>eyes</u> like a flame of <u>fire</u>… (Rev. 1:14)

D.   *Jesus' voice:* As a trumpet, He gathers His people, warns of judgment, and announces His return.

¹⁰A loud <u>voice</u>, as of a <u>trumpet</u>…¹⁵His voice as the <u>sound of many waters</u>… (Rev. 1:10, 15)

E.   *Jesus' hair:* Jesus' head and hair are white as wool and snow, indicating the Father's glory. God's white garments and hair speak of His eternal existence, purity, and wisdom (Dan. 7:9).

¹⁴His head and hair were <u>white like wool</u>, as <u>white as snow</u>… (Rev. 1:14)

F.   *Jesus' garments:* Jesus is seen as our high priest, being clothed in priestly robes. Jesus, the glorious Son of Man, is also a sympathetic, tender high priest who understands us (Heb. 4:15).

¹³…clothed with a <u>garment down to the feet</u> and girded…with a <u>golden band</u>. (Rev. 1:13)

G.   *Jesus' right hand:* Jesus holding the seven stars, or His leaders, speaks of His promise to anoint, direct, and protect them. He is tender towards us even when we feel inadequate.

¹⁶In His right hand <u>seven stars</u>…²⁰The <u>seven stars</u> are the <u>angels</u> [messengers]… (Rev. 1:16, 20)

H.   *Jesus' feet and sword:* As a King, He puts all things under His feet and uses His sword to remove all resistance to His rule (Rev. 19:15–16). His Word is compared to a sword (Eph. 6:17).

¹⁵His <u>feet</u> were like fine brass…¹⁶Out of His <u>mouth</u> went a sharp two-edged <u>sword</u>… (Rev. 1:15–16)

I.   *Jesus' countenance:* Jesus' glorious radiance exhilarates the saints and destroys His enemies.

¹⁶His <u>countenance</u> was like the sun shining in its strength. (Rev. 1:16)

J.   *A-R-K:* We apply the truths about Jesus in Revelation 1 to our lives in three ways:

1.   *Agreement:* Make *declarations of agreement* to Jesus as the faithful witness. Pray, "Jesus, You are the faithful witness. You took a stand with courage and love. I believe You."

2.   *Revelation:* "Reveal Yourself to me and show me Your glory as the faithful witness."

3.   *Keep the prophecy:* Respond in faith and obedience to the specific truth of Jesus as the faithful witness. Pray, "I will stand for truth regardless what it costs me. Help me."

⁷"Blessed is he who <u>keeps the words</u> of the prophecy of this book." (Rev. 22:7)

Session 4: The Seven Churches—Called to Overcome (Rev. 2–3)

I. REVIEW: MESSAGE OF THE BOOK OF REVELATION

A. The book of Revelation is called the **revelation of Jesus** because it reveals the majesty of His heart and leadership in His plan to transition the earth to the age to come. Secondly, it is a book about events that take place in His end-time plan to purify the Church, bring in the harvest, and replace evil governments. The main point in Revelation is to <u>reveal the Man behind the plan</u>.

¹*The <u>Revelation of Jesus Christ</u>, which God gave Him [Jesus] to show His servants—<u>things</u> which must shortly take place. And He sent and <u>signified it by His angel</u> to…John. (Rev. 1:1)*

B. In Revelation 1–3, John shared a vision highlighting **30 descriptions** of Jesus' majesty, ministry, and personality, and **18 eternal rewards**. Each description and reward communicates a specific insight into Jesus that is necessary in equipping the Church to overcome compromise. We identify the 30 descriptions from Jesus' titles, names, appearance, actions, and clothing.

C. Revelation 1 and Revelation 19 are two of the most glorious descriptions of Jesus in the Bible. They describe *who He is* (how He thinks and feels) and *what He does* in His end-time plan.

D. Jesus will come *only* in the context of a prepared Bride walking in deep unity with the Spirit.

⁷*"For the marriage of the Lamb has come, and His wife has <u>made herself ready</u>." (Rev. 19:7)*

E. We must understand Jesus' message to the seven churches. It is His instruction on what the overcoming Church looks like. In Revelation 1–3, we see truths that Jesus wants emphasized to prepare His Church to be used in the greatest revival in history—the end-time revival. He gave us a picture of what He wants in the Church and defined the quality of love and spiritual maturity that will be needed for the Church to overcome in the face of great temptation and persecution.

II. HOW TO APPLY THE 7 LETTERS: 4 WAYS

A. <u>*Individually:*</u> the letters were written to inspire wholeheartedness in individuals.

B. <u>*Historically:*</u> the letters were first written to seven actual churches in John's generation to address their spiritual condition and to encourage them. Some see parallels of the spiritual conditions of the seven churches of Asia in the first century to the spiritual conditions of successive periods in church history. I am not sure this can be substantiated, but it is possible.

C. <u>*Universally:*</u> the letters were to benefit all churches throughout 2,000 years of church history. They were written to equip local churches to walk *corporately* in these truths together. Jesus spoke to individuals ("he" who has an ear), then applied it to a group ("churches").

⁷*"He who has an ear, let <u>him</u> hear what the Spirit says to the <u>churches</u>." (Rev. 2:7)*

D. <u>*Eschatologically:*</u> to prepare the end-time Church for the events seen in Revelation 6–19.

III. STUDYING THE 7 LETTERS: COMMON ELEMENTS

A. ***Revelation of Jesus:*** each message begins with Jesus calling attention to specific aspects of His majesty that were needed to equip them to overcome persecution and specific temptations.

B. ***Historical context:*** it is important to gain information about the situation with which each church was challenged politically, economically, and spiritually. Jesus strategically selected these seven, knowing they would give prophetic insight into preparing the end-time Church.

C. ***Affirmation for faithfulness:*** Jesus gave His affirmations before His corrections (Ephesus, Pergamos, and Thyatira). Two churches received no affirmation (Sardis and Laodicea).

D. ***Corrected for compromise:*** Jesus highlighted six temptations. They are immorality and idolatry (Rev. 2:14, 20), holding the doctrine of the Nicolaitans (Rev. 2:15), leaving their first love (Rev. 2:4), having a name of being spiritually alive but being spiritually dead (Rev. 3:1), and lukewarmness (Rev. 3:16). Two churches did not receive correction from Jesus (Smyrna and Philadelphia). The compromises He emphasized most were immorality, idolatry, and passivity.

E. ***Exhortation to respond:*** Jesus gave actions that He required them to take, often with an element of warning. He warned them the most about *fear* (of persecution and rejection).

F. ***Promise for overcomers:*** Jesus gave promises as incentive for diligent faithfulness to Him. Most of them have their greatest fulfillment in the Millennium. Insight into them helps equip us to stand in pressure. Jesus promised us 18 eternal rewards in Revelation 2–3 (2:7, 10, 17, 26; 3:5, 12, 21).

   1. Jesus taught on eternal rewards more than any other man in the Scripture. Here Jesus mentioned 18 rewards that equip His people to persevere by being anchored in eternity with confidence that our choices matter to such a degree that they will be rewarded.

   2. Jesus was speaking to believers who had already received the free gift of salvation. He was calling believers to live in a way to receive heavenly rewards.

   3. Salvation or justification is a free gift given to us. It is based on Jesus' worthiness (Eph. 2:8–9). Heavenly rewards are given to us according to our works or our response of gratitude to Jesus for giving us so great a salvation. There will be a difference in the measure of glory of each one's reward (1 Cor. 15:41–42).

G. The exhortation that Jesus repeated the most in His earthly ministry was the call to have ***ears to hear what the Spirit is saying***. This is written 16 times (8x in the gospels and 8x in Revelation: Mt. 11:15; 13:9, 43; Mk. 4:9, 23; 7:16; Lk. 8:8; 14:35; Rev. 2:7, 11, 17, 29; 3:6, 13, 22; 13:9).

   [7]***"He who has an ear, let him hear what the Spirit says to the churches." (Rev. 2:7)***

H.   "The angel of the church" refers to the apostolic leader over each church. The word angel is *angelos* in Greek. The word refers to an angelic or human messenger (Lk. 7:24, 27; 9:52). It was translated *messenger* when referring to John the Baptist (Mt. 11:10). The messenger was responsible to guard the message and not let it be distorted through compromise, fear, or neglect.

IV.   EPHESUS: RETURNING TO OUR FIRST LOVE (REV. 2:1–7)

A.   The primary message: the church of Ephesus was affirmed for their diligent work and perseverance in standing for truth, but corrected for lacking love for Jesus in their labors.

B.   Jesus' revelation of Himself: He holds the seven stars and walks in the midst of His people. He holds, supports, directs, protects, and anoints His servants and is deeply involved with His churches, protecting those who walk with Him as Adam walked with God in the garden of Eden.

> *[1]To the angel of the church of <u>Ephesus</u> write, "These things says He who holds the seven stars in His right hand, who walks in the midst of the seven golden lampstands." (Rev. 2:1)*

C.   Jesus affirmed their perseverance in their labor and standing for truth (v. 2, 6).

> *[2]"I know your works, your labor, your patience [perseverance], and that you cannot bear those who are evil. And you have tested those who say they are apostles and are not, and have found them liars." (Rev. 2:2)*

D.   Jesus corrected them for neglect in cultivating their first love for God (v. 4). He exhorted them to remember, repent, and act in the ways that they did in their former days (v. 5). He promised them a place "in the midst" of the paradise in the New Jerusalem (v. 7).

> *[4]"Nevertheless I have this against you, that you have left your first love. [5]<u>Remember</u> therefore from where you have fallen; <u>repent</u> and <u>do</u> the first works…[7]To him who overcomes I will give to eat from the tree of life, which is <u>in the midst</u> of the Paradise of God." (Rev. 2:4–7)*

V.   SMYRNA: FAITHFULNESS IN SUFFERING (REV. 2:8–11)

A.   The primary message: the church of Smyrna was called to continue to walk in the grace of fearlessness and faithfulness in persecution.

B.   Jesus' revelation of Himself: He is the First, the source of all blessing, and the Last, in seeing the end of all things. Therefore He can assure us that all His promises will come to pass. As a man, He was dead and came to life; thus He suffered in being killed in a cruel way. He understood what they went through and prevailed with power, knowing the way to full victory.

> *[8]To the angel of the church in <u>Smyrna</u> write, "These things says the First and the Last, who was dead, and came to life." (Rev. 2:8)*

C.   Jesus affirmed their love and perseverance in persecution (v. 9) and exhorted them not to fear (v. 10). He gave them no correction and promised them authority over the nations (v. 11).

> *[9]"I know your works, tribulation, and poverty (but you are rich)…[10]Do not fear any of those things which you are about to suffer. Indeed, the devil is about to throw some of you into*

prison…Be faithful until death, and I will give you the crown of life. [11]…He who overcomes shall not be hurt by the second death." (Rev. 2:8–11)

VI.   PERGAMOS: A CHURCH WITH COMPROMISE (REV. 2:12–17)

A.   The primary message: the church of Pergamos was affirmed for their faithfulness in not yielding to fear in persecution and called to refuse to yield to sin in the midst of a perverse culture. They were to stand up against false teaching of Balaam that allowed immorality and idolatrous feasts.

B.   Jesus' revelation of Himself: He has the two-edged sword (v. 12). This emphasizes His zeal to intervene against the evil government of the Roman Empire as well as sin in the church. There are five references to Jesus' sword (Rev. 1:16; 2:12, 16; 19:15, 21). Four times it refers to the sword of His mouth. When He speaks, the Spirit releases the sword of judgment on His enemies.

[12]*To…the church in Pergamos write, "These things says He who has the sharp two-edged sword." (Rev. 2:12)*

C.   Jesus affirmed their faithfulness in not yielding to fear in the midst of persecution (v. 13).

[13]*"I know your works…you hold fast to My name, and did not deny My faith even in the days in which Antipas was My faithful martyr, who was killed among you, where Satan dwells." (Rev. 2:13)*

D.   He corrected their compromise in tolerating immorality and idolatry (v. 14). He exhorted them to repent (v. 16) and promised them hidden manna and a white stone (v. 17).

[14]*"But I have a few things against you, because you have there those who hold the doctrine of Balaam, who taught…to eat things sacrificed to idols, and to commit sexual immorality… [16]Repent, or else I will…fight against them with the sword of My mouth. [17]…To him who overcomes I will give some of the hidden manna to eat. And I will give him a white stone, and on the stone a new name written which no one knows except him who receives it." (Rev. 2:14–17)*

E.   Augustine said, "Lust yielded to becomes a habit, and a habit not resisted becomes necessity [addiction]."

VII.   THYATIRA: COMMITTED, YET TOLERATING IMMORALITY (REV. 2:18–29)

A.   The primary message: the church of Thyatira was commended for their love and ministry, yet warned not to tolerate Jezebel who promoted immorality and idolatry.

B.   Jesus' revelation of Himself: the Son of God with eyes of fire and feet like brass. Being the Son of God emphasizes His deity and power to withstand Jezebel. His eyes being like fire speak of His love for His people and His judgment or zeal to remove all that hinders love. His feet like brass speak of judgment against sin. He promises to tread down all that is identified with Jezebel.

[18]*To…the church in Thyatira write, "These things says the Son of God, who has eyes like a flame of fire, and His feet like fine brass." (Rev. 2:18)*

C.   Jesus releases either the *fire of grace* or the *fire of judgment*, depending on how His people respond to His leadership.

D.   Jesus affirmed their ministry, love, service, faith, and perseverance in persecution (v. 19).

[19]"I know your works, love, service, faith, and your patience [perseverance]…" (Rev. 2:19)

E.   He corrected their toleration of idolatry and immorality, or lacking in moral purity, (v. 20) and warned of His discipline (v. 21–23). To overcomers, He promised power over the nations (v. 26).

[20]"Nevertheless I have a few things against you, because you allow [tolerate] that woman Jezebel… to teach and seduce My servants to commit sexual immorality…[21]I gave her time to repent of her sexual immorality, and she did not repent. [22]Indeed I will cast her into a sickbed, and those who commit adultery with her into great tribulation, unless they repent…[23]I will kill her children with death…[26]He who overcomes, and keeps My works until the end, to him I will give power over the nations…" (Rev. 2:20–26)

F.   Believers are sometimes made sick and even die under God's judgment. God's discipline includes Satan being permitted to make the unrepentant sick (1 Cor. 5:1–5; 11:30–32).

[30]For this reason many are weak and sick among you, and many sleep [died]. [31]If we…judge ourselves, we would not be judged. [32]But when we are judged, we are chastened [disciplined] by the Lord, that we may not be condemned [go to hell] with the world. (1 Cor. 11:30–32)

[1]It is actually reported that there is sexual immorality among you…[5]deliver such a one to Satan for the destruction of the flesh, that his spirit may be saved in the day of the Lord Jesus. (1 Cor. 5:1–5)

VIII.   SARDIS: REPUTATION WITHOUT SPIRITUAL SUBSTANCE (REV. 3:1–6)

A.   The primary message: the church of Sardis was called to repent of their spiritual passivity.

B.   Jesus' revelation of Himself: He has the seven Spirits of God and the seven stars. He will release the seven-fold diverse ministries of the Spirit to them (Isa. 11:2) and will hold His people in His hands, which speaks of being deeply involved in their life and ministry.

[1]To the angel of the church in Sardis write, "These things says He who has the seven Spirits of God and the seven stars…" (Rev. 3:1)

C.   Jesus gave them no affirmation, but corrected their spiritual passivity and lukewarmness (v. 1). They had a reputation of being spiritually alive, but lacked a sense of the Spirit's presence and inspiration in their life. He exhorted them to be watchful and strengthen the things that remained (v. 2) as they remembered and repented (v. 3). He promised them white garments, not to blot their names out of the Book of Life, and to confess them before the Father (v. 5).

[1]"I know your works, that you have a name that you are alive, but you are dead. [2]Be watchful, and strengthen the things which remain…[3]Remember therefore how you have received and heard; hold fast and repent…[5]He who overcomes shall be clothed in white garments, and I

will not blot out his name from the Book of Life; but I will confess his name before My Father…" (Rev. 3:1–5)

IX.   PHILADELPHIA: FAITHFULNESS UNTO ETERNAL REWARDS (REV. 3:7–13)

A.   The primary message: the church of Philadelphia was affirmed for their faithfulness to Jesus.

B.   Jesus' revelation of Himself: He who is holy and true and who has the key of David. Jesus is holy or transcendent (infinitely superior to all). Thus He is worth whatever it costs to love and obey Him. He is true, reliable in His extravagant promises (Rev. 3:12). He has the key of David, which includes being the heir of all the promises that God gave David, having great authority.

> *[7]To…the church in __Philadelphia__ write, "These things says He who is holy, He who is true, He who has the key of David, He who opens and no one shuts…" (Rev. 3:7)*

C.   Jesus affirmed their faithfulness to obey in the face of temptation and great persecution (v. 8). He gave them no correction, but exhorted them to hold fast or to continue to persevere (v. 11). He promised to make them a pillar in God's temple and to write on them God's name (v. 12).

> *[8]"I know your works…for you…have __kept My word__, and have not denied My name…[11]Hold fast what you have, that no one may take your crown. [12]He who __overcomes__, I will make him a pillar in the temple of My God…I will write on him the name of My God and the name of the city of My God, the New Jerusalem…" (Rev. 3:8–12)*

X.   LAODICEA: SPIRITUAL PRIDE AND LUKEWARMNESS (REV. 3:14–22)

A.   The primary message: the church of Laodicea was promised deeper fellowship with God and authority in His eternal kingdom *if* they zealously repented of their lukewarmness.

B.   Jesus' revelation of Himself: He is the Amen because His promises are sure and the Faithful Witness because what He speaks is reliable as He revealed their failures (v. 15–17) and promises (v. 20–21). He is the beginning of creation, being the *First Cause* and having all authority over it.

> *[14]To the angel of the church of the Laodiceans write, "These things says the Amen, the Faithful and True Witness, the Beginning of the creation of God." (Rev. 3:14)*

C.   Jesus gave them no affirmation for their faithfulness. He corrected their lukewarmness and spiritual pride (v. 15–17). He exhorted them to buy gold refined by fire (v. 18) and promised them deep fellowship with God and authority over the nations (v. 20–21).

> *[16]"…because you are lukewarm, and neither cold nor hot, I will vomit you out of My mouth. [17]Because you say, 'I am rich, have become wealthy, and have need of nothing'—and do not know that you are wretched, miserable, poor, blind, and naked…[19]be zealous and repent. [20]Behold, I stand at the door and knock. If anyone…opens the door, I will come in to him…[21]To him who overcomes I will grant to sit with Me on My throne…" (Rev. 3:16–21)*

Session 5: The Father's Throne and Jesus' Exaltation (Rev. 4–5)

I. THE MAJESTY OF THE FATHER'S THRONE: GUARANTEES JESUS' EXALTATION

A. In Revelation 4–5, John described the majesty of the Father's royal court in heaven and the glorious occasion when Jesus took a scroll from the Father indicating His right to rule the earth.

B. Revelation 4 gives us the most detailed description of God's beauty in the Scripture. I refer to this chapter as the "beauty realm of God."

C. Revelation 5 gives us insight in the Father's plan to exalt Jesus as a human king over the earth. The primary theme in the book of Revelation is Jesus coming back as King to rule the nations.

D. God's vast majestic resources (Rev. 4) are committed to establishing His plan for Jesus (Rev. 5).

II. THE FATHER'S HEAVENLY COURT: THE BEAUTY OF GOD (REV. 4)

A. Revelation 4:2–7 outlines four categories of God's beauty, each with three themes, totaling 12.

²I was in the Spirit; and behold, a throne set in heaven, and One sat on the throne. ³And He who sat there was like a jasper and a sardius stone in appearance; and there was a rainbow around the throne, in appearance like an emerald. ⁴Around the throne were twenty-four thrones…I saw twenty-four elders sitting…in white robes; and they had crowns of gold… ⁵From the throne proceeded lightnings, thunderings, and voices. Seven lamps of fire were burning before the throne, which are the seven Spirits of God. ⁶Before the throne there was a sea of glass, like crystal…around the throne, were four living creatures… (Rev. 4:2–6)

1. The beauty of *God's Person*: how God looks, feels, and acts (Rev. 4:3)
2. The beauty of *God's Partners*: the Church enthroned, robed, and crowned (Rev. 4:4)
3. The beauty of *God's Power*: manifestations of power in lightning, thunder, voices (Rev. 4:5a)
4. The beauty of *God's Presence* (fire): on lamps, seraphim, and the sea (Rev. 4:5b–7; 15:2)

B. In Revelation 4:8–11, we see the governmental leaders of heaven worship God and declare His transcendent beauty (v. 8). They glory or boast with delight in God as they honor and thank Him.

⁸The four living creatures…do not rest day or night, saying: "Holy, holy, holy, Lord God Almighty, who was and is and is to come!" ⁹Whenever the living creatures give glory and honor and thanks to Him who sits on the throne…¹⁰the twenty-four elders fall down…and worship Him…and cast their crowns before the throne, saying: ¹¹"You [Father] are worthy, O Lord, to receive glory and honor and power; for You created all things…" (Rev. 4:8–11)

C. Their foundational hymn forever magnifies God's holiness (v. 8). There are 14 hymns in Revelation. To be holy means "to be totally separated from." God is separated from everything sinful; thus He is pure. God is also separated from everything created; thus He is transcendent or infinitely superior to all that exists. God's holiness points to His transcendent beauty.

III.   THE GRAND DRAMA IN HEAVEN (REV. 5:1–14)

A.   Revelation 5 describes Jesus' destiny on the earth as a Man. He is fully God and fully man. Because of His obedience to death, God highly exalted Him in heaven and on earth (Phil. 2:10). His exaltation is manifest *in part* on earth now, and *in fullness* in the Millennium.

> *[9]...God also has <u>highly exalted Him</u> and given Him the name which is <u>above every name</u>, [10]that at the name of Jesus every knee should <u>bow</u>, of those in heaven, and of <u>those on earth</u>... (Phil. 2:9–10)*

B.   Daniel prophesied that Israel's messiah would receive the leadership of the earth forever. David wrote of the Father's promise to give the leadership of the nations to Jesus (Ps. 2:8). This promise is fulfilled in the eyes of the nations *in part* in this age and *in fullness* in the Millennium.

> *[13]"...the Son of Man [Jesus], coming with the clouds of heaven! <u>He came</u> to the Ancient of Days [the Father]...[14]Then to Him was given...a kingdom, <u>that all peoples, nations, and languages should serve Him</u>. His dominion is an everlasting dominion..." (Dan. 7:13–14)*

> *[8]"'I [the Father] will give You [Jesus] <u>the nations</u> for Your inheritance...'" (Ps. 2:8)*

IV.   JESUS TAKES THE SCROLL FROM THE FATHER'S HAND (REV. 5)

A.   John saw a scroll in the Father's hand. Many see this scroll as representing the ***title deed*** of the earth and Jesus' ***action plan*** (Rev. 6–19) to bring in the harvest of all nations and to prepare the Church as a Bride to partner with Him in ruling the earth (Rev. 19:7–20:6) as He cleanses the earth of evil and replaces its governments so as to fill the earth with God's glory (Rev. 20–22).

> *[1]I saw in the right hand of Him [the Father] who sat on the throne a <u>scroll</u>...sealed with seven seals. [2]Then I saw a strong angel proclaiming..."Who is <u>worthy</u> to <u>open</u> the scroll and to loose its seals?"...[5]One of the elders said to me, "...the <u>Lion</u> of the tribe of Judah...has prevailed to <u>open the scroll</u> and to loose its seven seals." [6]...In the midst of the elders, stood a <u>Lamb</u> as though it had been slain, having <u>seven horns and seven eyes</u>, which are the seven Spirits of God...[7]He...<u>took the scroll</u> out of the right hand of Him...on the throne. (Rev. 5:1–7)*

B.   ***Open the scroll:*** Jesus will open the scroll and loose or break the seven seals (v. 2, 5). This includes releasing the judgments that are described in Revelation (Rev. 6–19).

C.   ***Taking the scroll:*** by taking the scroll, He accepted responsibility to cleanse and rule earth.

D.   ***Who is worthy:*** Jesus is the only man who was found worthy or deserving and capable to take the scroll from the Father. No other man is able to solve the problems of the nations.

E.   ***Lion and lamb:*** Jesus has the fierceness and fearlessness of a lion (v. 5) and the tenderness and humility of a lamb (v. 6). He will forever be a Jewish Man from the tribe of Judah (v. 5).

F.   ***Seven horns and eyes:*** Jesus is described as a lamb with seven horns, or all power, and seven eyes or all wisdom. Because He possesses all power and wisdom, He is qualified to open the scroll.

> *[6]...a Lamb...having <u>seven horns</u> and <u>seven eyes</u>, which are the seven Spirits of God. (Rev. 5:6)*

V.   JESUS IS WORTHY (REV. 5)

A.   The highest governmental council around God's throne consists of the living creatures (angelic) and the elders (human). They fell awestruck before the worthy Man and boldly proclaimed their agreement with the Father's decree to make Jesus the supreme leader of the whole earth forever!

⁸When He [Jesus] had __taken the scroll__, the four living creatures and the twenty-four elders fell down before the Lamb, each having a harp, and golden bowls __full of incense__, which are the prayers of the saints. ⁹And they sang a new song, saying: "__You are worthy__ to take the scroll, and to __open its seals__ [release end-times judgments]; for You were slain, and have redeemed us to God by Your blood [proved Your leadership and love] out of every tribe and tongue…¹⁰And have made us kings and priests to our God; and we shall reign on the earth." (Rev. 5:8–10)

1.   ___Sang a new song:___ a prophetic song indicating the changing of season in God's purpose. On earth there will be more and more expressions of this prophetic song released through prophetic singers as we get closer to the Lord's return.

2.   ___You were slain:___ when Jesus had all the glory, He laid it down for love and became poor for our sakes in becoming a man and taking our judgment so that we might become rich.

⁹You know the grace of our Lord Jesus Christ, that though He was rich, yet __for your sakes__ He became __poor__, __that you__ through His poverty might become __rich__. (2 Cor. 8:9)

B.   ___You are worthy:___ Jesus being worthy to be the supreme leader of the earth has three applications.

1.   ___Jesus deserves it___: He is worthy or deserving of the authority to be the supreme leader of the earth because He is our redeemer and creator. He has proven Himself by making every choice for love and righteousness.

2.   ___Jesus is capable___: He is able to open the seals or administrate God's judgments and rule the earth forever. He is able to drive evil off the earth and then reorganize and rule all the governments. No other man has the ability (wisdom, humility, and power) to lead all the resources of all the nations in a way that sustains love and righteousness forever. It is not amazing that God rules the earth, but that He gave all the authority to one Man.

3.   ___Jesus is worth it___: He is worthy of our wholehearted love—our *continual praise* of His beauty, our *confident trust* in His leadership, and *sacrificial obedience* to His will. As we see the worthiness of Jesus, we count all things loss in our pursuit to love Him (Phil. 3:8).

⁸I also count all things loss for the __excellence of the knowledge of Christ__… (Phil. 3:8)

4.   The devil seeks to stir up self-pity in us by telling us that we are getting a bad deal from God and that it is no longer worth the trouble to seek God with diligence. The devil tempts us to "*give up* (seeking God) and *give in* (to sin) because it is too hard."

C.   Father's promised to make Jesus preeminent in all things.

¹⁸He is the head of the body…that in __all things He may have the preeminence__. (Col. 1:18)

D.   Jesus' inheritance includes having the full authority over seven spheres of life: power, riches, wisdom, strength, honor, glory, and blessing. There are many aspects implied by each sphere. These are seven manifestations of His leadership and the response of the nations to Him.

> *12...saying with a loud voice: "__Worthy is the Lamb who was slain to __receive__ power and riches and wisdom, and strength and honor and glory and blessing!__" (Rev. 5:12)*

E.   The word *receive* is significant. In what sense does Jesus receive these? At His resurrection, He received authority as a Man from the Father to rule the earth (Eph. 1:20–23). He will receive the *full* obedience of all of His people in the Millennium. The kings will offer their national resources to Him. His people offer Him this response *in part* now and *fully* in the Millennium.

F.   **Power** (political): Jesus will publicly receive the political authority over all nations at His return. In the Millennium, the Father will establish Jesus as King over all nations, and all the kings will be saved and will base their governments on the Scriptures (Ps. 102:15; 138:4; 148:11; Isa. 62:2).

> *11Yes, __all kings__ shall __fall__ down before Him; __all nations__ shall serve Him. (Ps. 72:11)*

G.   **Riches** (financial): All the money and natural resources on earth will be openly seen as under Jesus' leadership in the Millennium. All the leaders of the nations will joyfully submit their riches to His leadership and worldwide plan (Isa. 60:5–13).

H.   **Wisdom** (intellectual): Jesus will use His great wisdom to bring every sphere of life to the fullness of the Father's plan (i.e., political, economic, family, agricultural, media, technology, environment, social institutions, etc.). He will have leadership over all the "intellectual property" forever. He will establish new leaders, laws, and policies in all the nations to bring every sphere of society to its fullness and fill the earth with God's glory.

I.   **Strength** (physical/emotional): The nations will love Jesus with all their strength or resources, which include their time, words, energy, and influence (Mk. 12:30). They will gladly offer to Jesus the fruit of their physical strength and labor with all their national resources. All the benefits of the labor force and human resources on the millennial earth will be submitted to Him.

J.   **Glory** (spiritual): Jesus will minister in the fullness of the supernatural realm of God's glory. The nations will submit to Jesus all that is gained by the glory of God operating in their lives.

K.   **Honor** (relational): Jesus will be the most praised, adored, respected, and listened-to man in all the nations. All in the nations will honor and love Him with their obedience (Eph. 6:1–2).

L.   **Blessing** (social) – all will fully cooperate with Jesus' leadership. By receiving such affirming cooperation from the nations, He will have the mightiest, largest, and most loyal, productive, unified, and joyful work force in history. The nations will bless all of His plans and policies.

Session 6: The Seals of Judgment and God's Protection (Rev. 6–7)

I.   INTRODUCTION TO THE SEVEN SEALS (REV. 5)

A.   Jesus took the scroll sealed with seven seals from the hand of the Father (5:7). It represents the *title deed* of the earth and the *action plan* required to cleanse the earth. One by one, Jesus will open each seal to release a terrifying judgment against the wicked.

> *⁷He [Jesus] came and <u>took the scroll</u> out of the right hand of Him [Father]…⁹And they sang a new song, saying: "You are worthy to <u>take the scroll</u>, and to <u>open its seals</u>…" (Rev. 5:7–9)*

B.   The seven seals are *literal* (not symbolic), *future* (their fulfillment is still in the future), *progressive* (increasing in intensity), and *numbered* (released in a sequential order).

C.   One's view of the timing in which Jesus will open the seals is one interpretive key to Revelation. I believe Jesus has not yet opened the first seal—the bowls of prayer must be full.

> *⁸When He [Jesus] had taken the scroll…the twenty-four elders fell down…each having a harp, and golden bowls <u>full of incense</u>, which are the prayers of the saints. (Rev. 5:8)*

D.   In the generation in which the Lord returns, God will shake all nations to judge the kingdom of darkness, purify the Church, and bring in the great harvest including the salvation of Israel. This process will been seen in the beginning of birth pangs and in the release of the seal, trumpet, and bowl judgments, culminating in the kings dying at Armageddon (Rev. 19:19).

> *⁶"'…<u>I will shake heaven and earth</u>, the sea and dry land; ⁷and <u>I will shake all nations</u>, and they [unbelievers] <u>shall come</u> to the Desire of All Nations [Jesus]…' says the LORD."*
> *(Hag 2:6–7)*

E.   The seven seals will escalate the process of the Lord shaking all the nations by bringing judgment to the kingdom of darkness (the harlot Babylon Rev. 17) and purifying the Church, while creating the optimum context for many to be saved (the end-time harvest).

F.   The seven seals are released by Jesus, the Lamb of God (5:5; 6:1, 3, 5, 7, 9, 12; 8:1).

> *¹I saw <u>when the Lamb</u> [Jesus] <u>opened</u> one of the seals; and I heard one of the four living creatures saying with a voice like thunder, "<u>Come</u> and <u>see</u>." (Rev. 6:1)*

G.   *Come and see:* Four times John was exhorted to "come and see" (6:1, 3, 5, 7). He was to *come*, or draw closer to God, to position his heart to understand and then to *see*, or to pay attention. We must also "come and see" so that we have understanding to agree with Him in that day.

> *¹⁷Your eyes will <u>see the King in His beauty</u>…¹⁸Your heart will <u>meditate on terror</u>: "Where is the scribe? Where is he who weighs? Where is he who counts the towers?" (Isa. 33:17–18)*

H.   *Principle of judgment:* God's end-time judgments will remove all that hinders love. He will use the least severe means to reach the greatest number at the deepest level of love without violating anyone's free will.

I.   God's judgments against the wicked in the first four seals result from God taking His *restraining hand off* evil men, allowing them to sin in an unrestrained way against one another. The Antichrist will act violently against the nations, including the harlot Babylon (Rev. 17:16).

1.   The first four seals are brought about by the actions of sinful men.

2.   The fifth, sixth, and seventh seals involve supernatural actions from heaven.

J.   Each seal naturally leads to the unfolding of the next seal. For example, the release of the Antichrist in the first seal (Rev. 6:2) leads to a World War in the second seal, which in turn causes famine and economic crisis in the third seal, followed by death and disease, etc.

II.   **FIRST SEAL: ANTICHRIST'S POLITICAL AGGRESSION (6:1–2)**

A.   The opening of the first seal speaks of the Antichrist's political aggression (6:1–2).

¹I saw when the Lamb opened one of the seals; and I heard one of the four living creatures saying… "Come and see." ²And I looked, and behold, a white horse. He who sat on it had a bow; and a crown was given to him, and he went out conquering and to conquer. (Rev. 6:1–2)

B.   *White:* The color white symbolizes righteousness because the Antichrist's reign will initially appear righteous. He will be the counterfeit to Jesus who rides a white horse with truth (19:11).

C.   *Bow:* The Antichrist's rule will initially be gained by an "*arrowless bow.*" This speaks of his bloodless victories or peaceful conquest using deceptive diplomacy. The rider is pictured as ready to go to war on a horse with a bow in hand. A bow speaks of *striking at a distance.* Since there are no arrows, it is commonly understood as a *threat of war,* without war breaking out yet.

D.   *Crown:* the Antichrist wears a crown as a symbol of his political authority (13:1–2, 7).

1.   The Antichrist will receive authority, or permission, to act from God. Jesus possesses all authority (Mt. 28:18). He will give the Antichrist a limited sphere to act for 3½ years.

⁷And authority was given him [Antichrist] over every…nation. (Rev. 13:7)

¹⁸"All authority has been given to Me in heaven and on earth." (Mt. 28:18)

¹There is no authority except from God…the authorities that exist are appointed by God…⁴he is God's minister, an avenger to execute wrath on him who practices evil. (Rom. 13:1, 4)

2.   Satan and sinful leaders will also give their authority to the Antichrist (13:2).

²…The dragon [Satan] gave him his power, his throne, and great authority. (Rev 13:2)

E.   Through the Antichrist, God will judge the harlot Babylon for murdering the saints (17:6, 16).

III.   SECOND SEAL: WORLD WAR (6:3–4)

A.   The opening of the second seal speaks of the release of the final world war (6:3–4).

> *³When He opened the second seal, I heard the second living creature saying, "Come and see." ⁴Another horse, <u>fiery red</u>, went out. And it was granted to the one who sat on it to <u>take peace from the earth</u>, and that people should <u>kill</u> one another; and there was given to him a <u>great sword</u>. (Rev. 6:3–4)*

B.   ***Great sword:*** This sword speaks of extreme forms of bloodshed coming from war and violence. The Antichrist will start by using an "arrowless bow" (6:2), and then he will use a "great sword."

C.   ***Take peace from the earth:*** The context for the breaking of the seals is counterfeit world peace (1 Thes. 5:3), which will end with the opening of the second seal and the abomination of desolation. God will take peace from the nations made drunk by the great Harlot (17:6, 16).

> *³For when they say, "<u>Peace and safety!</u>" then <u>sudden destruction</u> comes upon them, as labor pains upon a pregnant woman. And they shall not escape. (1 Thes. 5:3)*

D.   The Antichrist will make a peace treaty with many nations for seven years and then break it.

> *²⁷"He [Antichrist] shall <u>confirm a covenant</u> [peace treaty] with many for <u>one week</u> [seven years]; but <u>in the middle</u> of the week [seven years] he shall bring an end to sacrifice and offering. And on the wing of abominations shall be one who makes desolate…" (Dan. 9:27)*

IV.   THIRD SEAL: FAMINE AND ECONOMIC CRISIS (6:5–6)

A.   The opening of the third seal speaks of releasing famine and economic crisis (6:5–6). This famine and economic collapse will follow the world war seen in the second seal (6:4).

> *⁵When He opened the third seal, I heard the third living creature say, "Come and see." So I looked, and behold, a <u>black horse</u>, and he who sat on it had a <u>pair of scales</u> in his hand. ⁶And I heard a voice in the midst of the four living creatures saying, "A quart of wheat for a <u>denarius</u>, and three quarts of barley for a denarius; and do not harm the oil and the wine." (Rev. 6:5–6)*

B.   ***Pair of scales:*** This speaks of an economic crisis. The greatest economic pressures and the most severe famine in history are yet to come against the nations who embrace the ways of the Harlot.

C.   ***Denarius:*** A denarius was equivalent to wages for one day's work.

   1.   A quart of wheat is the amount that one man would eat for one day on a minimal diet.

   2.   The economic crisis will cause one's earning power to be reduced to working all day to afford food for one person for one day. This represents about 10 times less buying power than in the world today.

D.   ***Wheat and barley:*** Wheat is superior in taste and nutrition to barley. Barley, an inferior grain, will be three times cheaper than the price of wheat.

V.   FOURTH SEAL: DEATH TO ONE-FOURTH OF THE EARTH'S PEOPLE (6:7–8)

A.   The opening of the fourth seal speaks of the death of one-fourth of the earth's population (6:7–8).

> *7When He opened the fourth seal, I heard the voice of the fourth living creature saying, "Come and see." 8So I looked, and behold, a <u>pale horse</u>. And the name of him who sat on it was <u>Death</u>, and <u>Hades</u> followed with him. And power was given to them over a <u>fourth</u> of the earth, to kill with <u>sword</u>, with <u>hunger</u>, with <u>death</u>, and by the <u>beasts</u> of the earth. (Rev. 6:7–8)*

B.   *Pale horse:* This is literally pale green or ashen. It is the color of death or the decay of a corpse.

C.   *Death and Hades:* Death is what happens to the physical body, which goes to the grave. Hades is the prison where the departed spirit of an unbeliever goes before going to the lake of fire after the Millennium.

D.   *A fourth:* John saw one-fourth of the world's population being killed by the sword, hunger, death (pestilence), and wild beasts. These are similar to the four judgments that Ezekiel referred to as "God's four severe judgments" (Ezek. 5:17; 14:21).

> *21"How much more it shall be when I send <u>My four severe judgments</u> on Jerusalem—the <u>sword</u> and <u>famine</u> and <u>wild beasts</u> and <u>pestilence</u>—to cut off man and beast from it?" (Ezek. 14:21)*

E.   *Hunger:* the starvation seen in the third seal will continue to escalate in the fourth seal.

F.   *Death:* The second use of "death" in verse 8 is probably related to martyrdom, pestilence, or disease. Fatal diseases will increase greatly.

G.   *Wild beasts:* Hungry beasts will come out of the wild to the city looking for food. They will probably be seen roaming in the open seeking to devour people because of great hunger.

H.   *One-fourth:* Some estimate that the population of the earth in 2050 will be 10 billion people. One-fourth of this 10 billion is about 2.5 billion. Thus it is possible that the number of deaths will exceed 2 billion people, which is 50 times greater than the death total seen in World War II.

VI.   FIFTH SEAL: PRAYER RELEASING JUDGMENT (6:9–11)

A.   The opening of the fifth seal is related to the power of the prayer movement that will release great judgment on Antichrist's empire as seen in the trumpet judgments (Rev. 8–9).

> *9When He opened the fifth seal, I saw under the altar [altar of incense in heaven] the souls of those who had been <u>slain</u> for the word of God...10And they cried with a loud voice, saying, "How long, O Lord, holy and true, until You <u>judge and avenge</u> our blood on those who dwell on the earth?" 11Then a white robe was given to each of them; and it was said to them that they should rest a little while longer, until both <u>the number</u> of their fellow servants and their brethren, who would be killed [martyred] as they were, <u>was completed</u>. (Rev. 6:9–11)*

B.   The fifth, sixth, and seventh seals involve heavenly activity. The judgment of each seal increases in intensity. The fifth seal is more severe than the four that precede it. The shedding of the blood of the saints stirs up God's vengeance (Rev. 19:2) and fuels the prayer movement. This is one of the main turning points in the story line seen in the book of Revelation.

> *²"Righteous are His judgments…He has <u>avenged</u> on her the blood of His servants…"*
> *(Rev. 19:2)*

C.   *They cried:* The intensity of the prayer ministry in heaven at this time gives us insight into the intensity of the prayer ministry on earth. The Spirit who inspires intercession in heaven will inspire the same on earth with profound unity.

D.   *How long:* The prayer, "How long…" is the most recorded prayer in Scripture (Zech. 1:12; Ps. 6:3; 13:2; 74:10; 79:5; 80:4; 89:46; 90:13; 94:3; Dan. 8:13; 12:6–13). Here is prayer for justice on the Antichrist's cruelty, vindication of God's reputation, and deliverance of His people.

> *⁷"…will not God bring about <u>justice</u> for His elect who cry to Him day and night…⁸He will bring about <u>justice</u> for them quickly. However, when the <u>Son of Man comes</u>, will He find faith on the earth?" (Lk. 18:7–8 NASB)*

E.   *Vengeance:* This is not a cry for personal revenge, but that God would remove reprobates who oppress His people and hate His kingdom. They will long to see the Antichrist's cruelty stop.

F.   *O Lord, <u>holy</u> and <u>true</u>, until You judge and avenge our blood…:* Holy and true are two aspects emphasized (3:7) in context to God's judgments. As the saints lean into God's sovereignty with confidence in Jesus' goodness, they see that His judgments are *holy* for they do not violate love and they are *true* in judging the guilty with accurate information. God's judgments are neither too severe, nor too lenient, neither too early, nor too late, but are filled with holiness and truth.

G.   *Dwell on earth:* The saints will ask God to avenge their blood on those who *dwell on the earth.*

VII.   THE SIXTH SEAL: COSMIC DISTURBANCES (6:12–17)

A.   The opening of the sixth seal will release a great earthquake with signs in the heavens (6:12–17). This seal begins God's specific answer to this prayer of the martyrs in heaven. It is followed by the release of the trumpet and bowl judgments on the Antichrist's empire (Rev. 8–9; 16).

> *¹²He opened the sixth seal, and behold, there was a <u>great earthquake</u>; and the <u>sun</u> became black as sackcloth of hair, and the <u>moon</u> became like blood. ¹³And the <u>stars</u> of heaven fell to the earth…¹⁴Then the <u>sky receded</u> as a scroll when it is rolled up, and every mountain and island was moved out of its place. ¹⁵And the kings of the earth, the great men, the rich men, the commanders, the mighty men, every slave and every free man, <u>hid themselves</u> in the caves and in the rocks of the mountains, ¹⁶and said to the mountains and rocks, "Fall on us and <u>hide us</u> from the face of Him who sits on the throne and from the wrath of the Lamb! ¹⁷For the great day of His wrath has come, and who is able to stand?" (Rev. 6:12–17)*

B.   **Great earthquake:** There will be a great earthquake or a worldwide geophysical upheaval (Hag. 2:6; Heb. 12:26–28). Every mountain will be moved, rather than destroyed. No one could hide in a mountain if they were all destroyed. Mountains continue to exist in the seventh bowl (16:20).

C.   **Sun:** What causes the sun to become darkened? This will be a supernatural sign sent by God as well as possibly including the natural effects of ash and debris from volcanic eruptions or smoke.

D.   **Stars:** The stars can speak of asteroids and meteor showers hitting the earth. The Greek word for stars used here is *"aster"* from which we get the word *asteroid*. An *aster* refers to any shining mass in the sky, including stars, meteors, asteroids, any flaming debris, etc.

VIII. FIRST ANGELIC EXPLANATION: WHO CAN STAND? (7:1–17)

A.   The angelic explanations are like parenthetical sections that follow the chronological sections. They answer the tough questions such as *Why are God's judgments so severe?* and *What will happen to the saints?* They describe how God helps the saints and the Antichrist attacks them.

B.   Angelic explanation #1: God's people sealed for protection—physical and spiritual (7:1–17). This angelic explanation answers the question, "Who can stand?" affirming the security of God's people. God answered this cry by revealing that 144,000 Jewish believers will stand in victory (7:1–8) and Gentile martyrs (7:9–17) shall stand strong without wavering in persecution.

C.   John sees a divine sealing on His people that gives them physical and spiritual protection.

> *¹I saw <u>four angels</u> standing at the four corners of the earth, holding the four winds of the earth, that the wind should not blow on the earth…²I saw another angel ascending from the east, having the <u>seal of the living God</u>. And he cried with a loud voice to the four angels…³saying, "Do not harm the earth, the sea, or the trees till we have <u>sealed</u> the servants of our God on their foreheads." ⁴And I heard the number of those who were sealed. One hundred and forty-four thousand of all the tribes of the children of Israel were sealed. (Rev. 7:1–4)*

D.   The 144,000 servants of God give us a picture of victory. They receive a protective seal before God strikes the earth, sea, and trees (7:3). Israel received a protective mark on their doors that saved their firstborn. Others will be sealed for protection (9:4). The *Goshen principle* speaks of God protecting His people from judgment (Ex. 8:22–23; 9:4–6, 26; Ps. 91; Ezek. 9:6; Zeph. 2:3).

> *⁴They were commanded not to harm the grass of the earth, or any green thing, or any tree, but <u>only those men who do not have the seal of God</u> on their foreheads. (Rev 9:4)*

E.   Gentile believers (7:9–17) will also stand strong spiritually without wavering in persecution. The weakest saints can be spiritually protected if they ask the Lord for help.

> *⁹Behold, a <u>great multitude</u> which no one could number, of <u>all nations</u>, tribes, peoples, and tongues, <u>standing before the throne</u>…¹⁰saying, "Salvation belongs to our God…" ¹³Then one of the elders answered, saying to me, "<u>Who are these</u> arrayed in white robes, and where did they come from?" ¹⁴…he said to me, "These are the ones who come out of the <u>great tribulation</u>, and washed their robes…in the blood of the Lamb." (Rev. 7:9–14)*

Session 7: The Trumpet Judgments (Rev. 8–9)

I. **THE SEVENTH SEAL AND THE RELEASING OF THE TRUMPET JUDGMENTS (8:1–6)**

A. The seventh seal includes the release of fiery trumpet judgments on the Antichrist's empire in conjunction with the prayers of all the saints (8:1–6). The fifth seal (6:9–11) focuses on the prayer of the martyrs in heaven, and the seventh seal points to heavenly help that the prayer movement on earth receives in partnering with Jesus in the release of the trumpet judgments.

[1]When He opened the seventh seal, there was <u>silence in heaven</u> for about half an hour. [2]And I saw the seven angels who stand before God, and to them were <u>given seven trumpets</u>. [3]Then another angel, having a golden censer, came and stood at the altar. He was <u>given much incense</u>, that he should offer it <u>with the prayers of all the saints</u> upon the golden altar which was before the throne. [4]And the smoke of the incense, with the <u>prayers of the saints</u>, ascended before God from the angel's hand. [5]Then the angel took the censer, filled it with <u>fire</u> from the altar, and <u>threw it to the earth</u>. And there were noises, thunderings, lightnings, and an earthquake. [6]So the <u>seven angels who had the seven trumpets prepared themselves to sound</u>. (Rev. 8:1–6)

B. ***Silence in heaven:*** There will be a dreadful yet glorious silence in heaven for half an hour in anticipation of God's judgments as the seven angels prepare to release them (8:1). It is estimated that it took a priest about a half an hour to offer incense in the temple (Lev. 16:13; Lk 1:10, 21). There will also be silence on the earth in light of God's end-time judgments (Ps. 46:10; Hab. 2:20; Zeph. 1:7; Zech. 2:13).

C. An angel will be given much "heavenly" incense to offer with the prayers of the saints. This will provide a supernatural strengthening of the end-time prayer movement that results in releasing fire on earth with cosmic disturbances and an earthquake (8:3–5). The prayers of the saints are imperfect because of human weakness (Rom. 8:26). The only thing needed to be "added" to our prayers is the perfect intercession (incense) of Jesus, which may be what is given to the angel.

[26]...the Spirit also helps in <u>our weaknesses</u>. For <u>we do not know</u> what we should pray for... (Rom. 8:26)

[34]Christ...at the right hand of God, who also <u>makes intercession for us</u>. (Rom. 8:34)

D. ***Prayer of all the saints:*** The prayers of *all* the saints are both accumulated from history as well as accelerated in the generation in which the Lord returns. The end-time prayer movement will be the most powerful force on earth as it functions under the leadership of Jesus.

E. God's trumpet and bowl judgments are not released on the saints, but on the Antichrist's empire. They will destroy the resources of the Antichrist's armies. The trumpet and bowl judgments parallel the ten plagues of Egypt against Pharaoh (Ex. 7–12). The walls of Jericho fell after Joshua blew seven trumpets (Josh. 6) as a prophetic picture of the fall of the Antichrist kingdom.

F. As Moses released the plagues on Egypt through prayer, and as the first apostles released God's power through prayer in the book of Acts, so the praying Church will be involved with Jesus as He releases His judgment on the Antichrist. The miracles of Exodus and Acts will be combined and multiplied on a global level. The Old Testament prophets prophesied that miracles like those seen in Egypt in Moses' generation would occur in the end time (Mic. 7:15; cf. Isa. 10:22–25; 11:12–16; 30:30; Jer. 16:14–15; 23:7–8; Ezek. 38:22; Joel 2:30).

[15]"As in the days when you came out of…Egypt, <u>I will show them wonders.</u>" (Mic. 7:15)

*[12]"…the works that I do he will do also; and <u>greater works than these he will do…</u>"
(Jn. 14:12)*

G. I see the book of Revelation as being like an end-time book of Acts so that the saints worldwide may have a unified prayer focus in knowing the sequence of God's judgments on the Antichrist. It is like a *"canonized prayer manual"* that will equip the Church to partner with Jesus in prayer. Imagine hundreds of millions of saints unified with Jesus and one another. The end-time prayer movement will need the unified prayers of the entire body of Christ worldwide to release this measure of power against the Antichrist who will be the greatest oppressor in human history.

H. A primary theme in Revelation is God's judgment against the Antichrist's empire. A secondary theme is the Antichrist's persecution of the saints (12:12; 13:4, 8). In the Tribulation, the Church need not fear that they will be powerless victims. Rather, they will be operating in power under Jesus' leadership. Only 12 of the 403 verses (3%) in the book of Revelation refer to persecution.

I. ***Principle of judgment:*** God's end-time judgments are released to remove all that hinders love. The Lord will use the least severe means to reach the greatest number of people at the deepest level of love without violating anyone's free will.

J. Christianity is more about *relating to and partnering with Jesus* to see God's glory and kingdom released on the earth and to drive evil off the planet than it is about escaping hell. The Lord wants to release His purposes on earth in context to deep partnership with His beloved people.

K. The Lord told Moses to divide the sea rather than waiting for God to do it (Ex. 14:15–16), and He told Moses to speak to the rock to release God's provision of water from it (Num. 20:7–8).

[15]The LORD said to Moses, "<u>Why do you cry to Me?</u>… [16]But lift up your rod, and <u>stretch out your hand over the sea and divide it…</u>" (Ex. 14:15–16)

[7]The LORD spoke to Moses… [8]"…<u>Speak to the rock</u>…it will yield its water." (Num. 20:7–8)

II. THE RELEASE OF THE TRUMPET JUDGMENTS (8:6)

A. The trumpet judgments have a 3-fold purpose. First, to *hinder* the Antichrist empire's spread of evil and persecution by destroying their natural resources. Second, to *warn* unbelievers of increased judgment by God and rage from Satan, thus creating an optimum environment for people to get saved. Third, to *rally* the saints to pray with unity as they see the trumpets unfold.

[6]So the seven angels who had the seven trumpets <u>prepared</u> themselves to sound. (Rev. 8:6)

B.　The seven trumpets are *literal* (not symbolic), *future* (their fulfillment is still in the future), *progressive* (increasing in intensity), and *numbered* (released in a sequential order).

C.　They are *supernatural* acts of God released against the Antichrist's empire through nature (first four trumpets) and demons (fifth and sixth trumpets). I do not believe they are to be understood as merely *natural* acts portrayed in symbolic language.

D.　The trumpet judgments are "limited" to one-third as highlighted twelve times (8:7–12). In other words, they are warnings of more to come in the seven bowls (16:1–21). The limitation of the trumpets to a partial judgment warns and gives opportunities to repent.

E.　The *first four trumpets* punish the Antichrist's empire by destroying their natural resources that support life (yet without directly touching people). The *fifth and sixth trumpets* will directly afflict humans by demonic torment and then killing one-third of the human race.

F.　In the *first four seals*, God lifts restraints off humans so that they destroy one another's resources. In the *first four trumpets*, God will destroy the resources of Antichrist's empire.

G.　In the *fifth and sixth seals*, the heavens will be opened to release supernatural activity (6:9–11). In the *fifth and sixth trumpets*, God lifts His restraints off the demonic realm (9:1–21).

H.　The first five trumpets (8:7–12) parallel the plagues of Egypt. The first (8:7) parallels the seventh plague of hail with fire and blood (Ex. 9:22–26). The second and third (8:8–11) parallel the first plague of the Nile turning to blood (Ex. 7:19–25). The fourth (8:12) parallels the ninth plague of darkness (Ex. 10:21–23) and the fifth (9:1–11), the eighth plague of locusts (Ex. 10:12–20).

III.　THE FIRST FOUR TRUMPETS: DESTRUCTION OF NATURAL RESOURCES (8:7–12)

A.　The first four trumpets will destroy the resources of the Antichrist's empire (8:6–12), affecting the *environment* (trees, grass, sea, rivers, sky), *food supplies* (vegetation, meat, fish), *sea trade*, *water supplies*, and both *light and heat* (sun, moon, stars). Their purpose is to destroy, not kill.

B.　*First trumpet:* It will destroy food supplies by burning one-third of the earth's vegetation (8:7). A supernatural event, like a meteor storm, with hail and fire will burn the earth's trees and grass.

> *⁷The first angel sounded: And <u>hail and fire followed</u>, mingled with blood, and they were thrown to the earth. <u>A third of the trees were burned up</u>, and all green grass was burned up. (Rev. 8:7)*

C.　*Second trumpet:* It will destroy food supplies and sea trade (8:8–9). A huge burning object like a mountain will fall from heaven turning one-third of the sea into blood and destroying one-third of the sea and ships. Some see this as referring *only* to the Mediterranean Sea (18:18; Isa. 2:12–16). The second trumpet corresponds to the first plague of Egypt where the rivers became as blood, causing the fish to die and polluting the land (Ex. 7:14–25; Ps. 105:2, 9; 78:43–44).

> *⁸Then the second angel sounded: And something like a <u>great mountain</u> burning with fire was thrown into the sea, and a third of the <u>sea became blood</u>. ⁹And a third of the <u>living creatures in the sea died</u>, and a third of the <u>ships were destroyed</u>. (Rev. 8:8–9)*

D.   **Third trumpet:** It will poison one-third of the earth's fresh water supply (8:10–11). A great burning star or meteoric mass will fall from heaven poisoning fresh water (rivers and springs). The saints will be protected as they were during the Egyptian plague on the Nile (Ex. 7:14–25).

> [10] *Then the third angel sounded: And a* <u>*great star fell*</u>*…burning like a torch, and it fell on a third of the* <u>*rivers*</u> *and on the* <u>*springs of water.*</u> [11] *The name of the star is Wormwood. A third of the waters became wormwood, and many men died from the water, because it was made bitter. (Rev. 8:10–11)*

E.   **Fourth trumpet:** It will destroy light and heat by darkening one-third of the sun, moon, and stars (8:12). This supernatural work of God will affect heat, health, agriculture, navigation, etc. Our lack of understanding of how this will occur is not a sufficient reason to see this as symbolic. This trumpet corresponds to the ninth Egyptian plague from which Israel was spared (Ex. 10:23).

> [12] *Then the fourth angel sounded: And a third of the* <u>*sun was struck,*</u> *a third of the* <u>*moon,*</u> *and a third of the* <u>*stars,*</u> *so that a third of them were* <u>*darkened.*</u> *A third of the day did not shine, and likewise the night. (Rev. 8:12)*

> [21] *The LORD said to Moses, "Stretch out your hand toward heaven, that there may be* <u>*darkness*</u> *over the land of Egypt, darkness which may* <u>*even be felt.*</u>*"* [22] *…there was thick darkness in all the land of Egypt three days.* [23] *…But all the children of* <u>*Israel had light in their dwellings.*</u> *(Ex. 10:21–23)*

IV.   UNDERSTANDING THE FIFTH AND SIXTH TRUMPETS (REV. 9)

A.   The fifth and sixth trumpet judgments will release two demonic armies on the earth. In one sense, the demons come in response to the worship of their loyal demonized followers (13:8). In the fifth and sixth trumpets, God lifts His restraints off the demonic realm so that their hatred for humans is manifest. The demonic realm beneath the earth is opened, releasing them (9:1–21).

B.   Demons hate the people who worship them as much as they hate Christians—they hate them *all* because they were made in God's image. Satan is a murderer from the beginning (Jn. 8:44). He never changes. His hatred will not be openly seen on earth until the fifth and sixth trumpets. Many will be deluded in thinking that Satan will give them favor for their loyal service to him.

C.   People will be turned over to Satan to experience the terrors of his hatred in order to give them opportunity to repent before progressing in evil by taking the mark of the Beast, which will be blasphemy. God wants unbelievers to see the truth about Satan, but He will honor the choice of the wicked by turning them over to the sin they love (Rom. 1:24–28).

> [19] *Some…* [20] <u>*whom I delivered to Satan*</u> *that they may* <u>*learn not to blaspheme. (1 Tim. 1:19–20)*</u>

> [5] <u>*Deliver such a one to Satan*</u> *for the destruction of the flesh, that his spirit* <u>*may be saved*</u> *in the day of the Lord Jesus. (1 Cor. 5:5)*

> [24] *Therefore* <u>*God also gave them up*</u> *to uncleanness, in the lusts of their hearts, to dishonor their bodies…* [26] *For this reason* <u>*God gave them up*</u> *to vile passions…exchanged the natural use for what is against nature…* [28] <u>*God gave them over*</u> *to a debased mind… (Rom. 1:24–28).*

V.   **FIFTH TRUMPET: TORMENT BY DEMONIC LOCUSTS (9:1–11)**

A.   The fifth trumpet will release an army of demonic locusts who will inflict pain on people (9:4).

¹Then the fifth angel sounded: And I saw a <u>star fallen</u> [descended] from heaven to the earth. To him was given <u>the key to the bottomless pit</u>. ²And he opened the bottomless pit…³out of the smoke <u>locusts</u> came on the earth. And to them was given power, as the <u>scorpions</u> of the earth have power. ⁴They were commanded not to harm the grass of the earth…but only those men who do not have the <u>seal</u> of God on their foreheads. ⁵And they were <u>not</u> given authority to kill them, but to <u>torment them for five months</u>…like the torment of a <u>scorpion</u>…⁶In those days men will seek death and will not find it; <u>they will desire to die, and <u>death will flee from them</u>. (Rev. 9:1–6)

B.   ***Star fallen:*** The word for *fallen* here can be translated as *descended*. I see this as a good angel descending or coming down from heaven with the key to open the bottomless pit to judge the wicked. The activity of this angel parallels the actions of a good angel with the key to the bottomless pit to bind Satan (20:1). Jesus has all authority in the spiritual realm (1:18; 3:7).

C.   ***Opened the pit:*** Some demons are bound by chains (2 Pet 2:4; Jude 6) being kept or reserved to be instruments of God's end-time judgment to inflict torment on those who worship the Beast. The bottomless pit or the abyss (Greek) is a temporary prison for fallen angels who will be released in the end times. This passage implies a "huge shaft" extending from the earth's surface to the depths of the earth where demons are imprisoned. This "shaft" is currently sealed.

⁴For if God did not spare the angels who sinned, but cast them down to hell and delivered them into <u>chains</u> of darkness, to be <u>reserved for judgment</u>… (2 Pet. 2:4)

D.   ***Seal:*** The saints receive a seal resulting in them being protected from God's judgments (9:4).

³…to them was given power, as the <u>scorpions</u> of the earth have power. ⁴They were commanded not to harm the grass…but <u>only</u> those men who do not have the <u>seal of God</u>… (Rev. 9:3–4)

¹⁹I give you the <u>authority to trample on serpents and scorpions</u>, and over <u>all</u> the power of the enemy [physical and spiritual], and <u>nothing</u> shall by any means hurt you. (Lk. 10:19)

E.   ***Men will seek death:*** The anguish of a scorpion sting will drive people to such despair that they will seek suicide. This refers to the eighth plague—yet without inflicting pain (Ex. 10:12).

F.   John described this demonic locust army (9:7–11) by comparing them to horses prepared for battle wearing golden crowns with human faces. These locusts are supernatural, demonic beings, not natural locusts. They can distinguish between unbelievers and believers (who have God's seal). The details here include the names, rank, description, and torment of demons. I believe we are to interpret these details at face value. Satan's hierarchy includes a demonic king named *Abaddon* (Hebrew) or *Apollyon* (Greek) or *destroyer* (English).

⁷The <u>shape</u> of the locusts was like horses…on their <u>heads</u> were crowns of something like gold, and their <u>faces</u> were like the faces of men…¹¹They had as <u>king</u> over them the angel of the bottomless pit, whose name in Hebrew is Abaddon, but in Greek he has the name Apollyon. (Rev. 9:7, 11)

VI.   SIXTH TRUMPET: DEATH BY DEMONIC HORSEMEN (9:12–21)

A.   In the sixth trumpet, four demons will be released to lead a demonic cavalry to kill one-third of the human race. In the fifth trumpet, people will seek to die (9:6). Their prayer will then be answered as the demons they worship kill them. This parallels the tenth plague (Ex. 12:29–32).

> *[13]Then the sixth angel sounded: And I heard a voice from the <u>four horns of the golden altar</u> which is before God, [14]saying to the sixth angel who had the trumpet, "<u>Release the four angels</u> [fallen demonic beings] who are bound at the great river <u>Euphrates.</u>" [15]So the four angels, who had been prepared for the hour and day and month and year, were released to <u>kill a third of mankind.</u> [16]Now the number of the army of the horsemen was <u>two hundred million</u>... [17]I saw the horses in the vision: those who sat on them...out of their mouths came fire, smoke, and brimstone. [18]By these three plagues a <u>third of mankind was killed</u>... (Rev. 9:13–18)*

B.   The sixth trumpet will be commissioned by the angel who serves at the golden altar of prayer to release the four angels of death in answer to the end-time prayer movement (8:3–5; 9:13). The horns of the altar was a place of asylum to cry for mercy. Good angels are not bound, only evil angels (2 Pet. 2:4; Jude 6) until the end times to be released as instruments of judgment.

C.   God will commission them to kill one-third of the human race. They are demons *prepared* for a specific work of judgment in the end times. The four angels give leadership over part of the demonic army of 200 million horsemen. Possibly each commands 50 million demonic horsemen.

D.   The four primary demonic strongholds in society will be murder, sorcery, immorality, and theft (9:21). There will be more demonized people on earth than any time in history.

> *[20]The rest of mankind, who were not killed by these plagues, did not repent...[21]They did not repent of their <u>murders</u> or their <u>sorceries</u> or their <u>sexual immorality</u> or their <u>thefts</u>. (Rev. 9:20–21)*

E.   Sin will reach its greatest heights in history. The Antichrist's empire will be like a "corporate Pharaoh" with hardened hearts. Sin will become ripe (14:18; 17:4; 18:5). The wheat and the tares, or the righteous and the wicked, will mature together at the end of the age (Mt. 13:29–30). People will love sin, and the Antichrist and will deeply hate Jesus, the truth, and the saints.

> *[23]"In the latter time...when the <u>transgressors have reached their fullness</u>..." (Dan. 8:23)*

F.   Many in the nations will become very "spiritual" following right after a season of being very secular. Perversion will escalate, being dynamically connected to the spirit realm. Immorality will be more than sexual hedonism; rather it will express demon worship with a dark spirituality.

Session 8: Prophetic Ministry in the End Times (Rev. 10–11)

I. INTRODUCTION

A. Revelation 10:1–11:13 is an angelic explanation (parenthetical section) that follows after the worldwide crisis described in Revelation 9. Angelic explanations answer questions such as "What happens to the saints?" in the crisis described in the chronological section that it follows.

B. In the crisis in Revelation 9, demons will kill one-third of the earth, leaving many in deception and confusion. There will be more demonized people on earth than at any time in history. The earth will be dominated by four strongholds—murder, sorcery, immorality, and theft (Rev. 9:21).

[15]So the four angels…were released to kill a third of mankind…[20]The rest of mankind, who were not killed by these plagues, did not repent…that they should not worship demons… [21]They did not repent of their <u>murders</u> or their <u>sorceries</u> or their <u>sexual immorality</u> or their <u>thefts</u>. (Rev. 9:15, 20–21)

C. There will be many false signs at that time (Rev. 13:13; 16:14; 18:23; 19:20; cf. 2 Thes. 2:8–9).

[4]"Take heed that no one <u>deceives</u> you. [5]For many will come…and will <u>deceive</u> many…[11]Many false prophets will rise up and <u>deceive</u> many… [24]For false christs and false prophets will rise and show great signs and wonders to <u>deceive</u>, if possible, even the elect." (Mt. 24:4–5, 11, 24)

D. In this angelic explanation (Rev. 10:1–11:13), God assures His people that He will release prophetic direction and great power to help them. They will understand God's heart and plans.

1. In Revelation 10, God promised to release new, significant prophetic understanding that will help people avoid deception and overcome confusion.

2. In Revelation 11, the two witnesses will preach with great power and release God's judgments against the Antichrist's systems during the final 3½ years of this age.

E. There will be a great outpouring of the Spirit (Joel 2:28–32; Acts 2:17–21; Eph. 4:11–13; Rev. 11:10, 18; 16:6; 18:20, 24). All believers will receive prophetic dreams and visions, etc. The Lord released a "down payment" on Joel's prophecy on the day of Pentecost (Acts 2:16). Yet it was not completely fulfilled in Peter's generation. For example, the signs such as the sun and moon growing dark with blood, fire, and smoke did not occur. In Acts 2, the Spirit rested on only 120 believers in *one city*. The fullness of Joel's prophecy requires a *global dimension*.

F. One of the greatest needs in the end times will be the need for prophetic understanding (Jer. 23:20; 30:24; Dan. 11:33–35; 12:3, 9–10; Joel 2:28–29; Mal. 4:5; Mt. 17:11; Acts 2:17–18; Rev. 11:3–6; 3:18; 13:18; 17:9; cf. Isa. 28:19–23; 43:18–20; Dan. 9:22).

[33]Those of the <u>people who understand</u> shall instruct <u>many</u>…[35]And some of <u>those of understanding</u> shall fall [martyrdom], to refine them [believers], purify them, and make them white, until the time of the end; because it is still for the appointed time. (Dan. 11:33–35)

II.   THE GLORY OF THE MIGHTY ANGEL (REV. 10:1–3)

A.   John's description of a mighty angel with authority gives insight into aspects of God's glory that will be released in the end times. He saw three mighty angels in Revelation (5:2; 10:1; 18:2).

> *¹I saw still another __mighty__ angel…clothed with a __cloud__. And a __rainbow__ was on his head, his face was like the __sun__, and his feet like pillars of __fire__. ²He had a little book open in his hand. And he set his right __foot__ on the sea and his left foot on the land, ³and __cried__ with a loud voice, as when a lion roars. (Rev. 10:1–3)*

1. *Mighty angel:* the release of the might or power of the Spirit
2. *Robed in a cloud of glory:* the release of God's manifest glory
3. *Rainbow around his head:* the release of God's promises and mercy
4. *Face shines like the sun:* the release God's radiance and strength
5. *Feet are like pillars of fire:* the release of God's holy judgment to establish love
6. *Feet on the sea and land:* the release God's inheritance for His people
7. *Cries out like a roaring lion:* the release of prophetic prayer in the boldness of a lion

B.   The seven thunders prophecies (Rev. 10:2–4)

> *²He [mighty angel] had a __little book open__ in his hand…³When he cried out, __seven thunders uttered their voices__ [messages]. ⁴Now when the seven thunders uttered their voices, I was about to write; but I heard a voice…saying to me, "__Seal up the things which the seven thunders uttered, and do not write them.__" (Rev. 10:2–4)*

C.   This open little book in the angel's hand is not the same as the scroll taken by Jesus (Rev. 5:7). The little book may contain part of the prophetic information contained in the Father's scroll.

1.   An open book reveals that the contents in it are knowable. The angel may have read its contents to release the seven thunders.

2.   John understood the seven messages enough to be able to write them. He was told to seal them until the end times. This indicates that these seven prophetic messages will not be made known until the end times.

3.   When a book is "opened," it implies that its prophetic information is being made known. When it is "sealed," it implies that its information is kept private until later.

D.   This was similar to what happened to Daniel when he sealed up his prophesies (Dan. 12:4, 9).

> *⁴"Daniel…__seal the book__ until the time of the end…" ⁷…He [angel] held up his right hand…and __swore__ by Him who lives forever, that it shall be for a time, times, and half a time [3½ years]… ⁹"For the words are closed up and __sealed__ till the time of the end." ¹⁰…None of the wicked shall understand, but the __wise shall understand__. (Dan. 12:4–10)*

E.   Daniel 10–12 is a parallel passage to Revelation 10–13. Daniel sealed up prophetic information with an angel of similar glory and a similar oath related to the same 3½ years (Dan. 12:4–10).

III.   THE END-TIME RELEASE OF THE SEVEN THUNDER MESSENGERS

A.   The angel swore by God's person that there should be no more delay.

> *⁵The angel whom I saw…raised up his hand to heaven ⁶and <u>swore</u> by Him who lives forever and ever…that there <u>should be delay no longer</u>, ⁷but in the days of the sounding of the seventh angel, when he is about to sound, the <u>mystery of God</u> would be finished. (Rev. 10:5–7)*

     1.   *No more delay:* the second coming of Jesus is described in the next chronological section (Rev. 11:15).

> *⁵¹Behold, I tell you a <u>mystery</u>: We shall not all sleep, but we shall all be changed— ⁵²in a moment, in the twinkling of an eye, at the <u>last trumpet</u>. For the trumpet will sound, and the dead will be raised incorruptible, and we shall be changed. (1 Cor. 15:51–52)*

     2.   *The mystery of God finished:* includes Jesus returning to rule the earth with His people

> *¹⁵Then the <u>seventh angel sounded</u>: And there were loud voices in heaven, saying, "The kingdoms of this world have become the kingdoms of our Lord and of His Christ, and He shall reign forever and ever!" ¹⁸"…and the time of the dead, that they should be judged, and that You should reward Your servants the prophets and the saints…and should destroy those who destroy the earth." (Rev. 11:15, 18)*

B.   John had to assimilate fully the prophetic message that he had been given (Rev. 10:8–11).

> *⁸The voice which I heard from heaven…said, "Go, <u>take the little book</u> which is open in the hand of the angel…" ⁹So I went to the angel and said to him, "Give me the little book." And he said to me, "Take and <u>eat it</u>; and it will make your <u>stomach bitter</u>, but it will be as <u>sweet</u> as honey in your mouth." ¹⁰Then I took the little book out of the angel's hand and <u>ate it</u>, and it was as sweet as honey in my mouth. But when I had eaten it, my stomach became bitter. ¹¹And he said to me, "You must <u>prophesy again</u> about many peoples, nations, tongues, and kings." (Rev. 10:8–11)*

     1.   John ate the prophetic scroll similar to Ezekiel (Ezek. 2:10–3:3). The principle being taught is that God's messengers must take time to digest God's prophetic purposes.

> *¹"Son of man…<u>eat this scroll</u>, and go, <u>speak</u> to the house of Israel." ²So I opened my mouth, and He caused me to <u>eat that scroll</u>. ³And He said to me, "Son of man, feed…and <u>fill your stomach with this scroll</u>…" ⁴Then He said to me, "…go to…Israel and <u>speak with My words</u> to them." (Ezek. 3:1–4)*

     2.   John was to eat it and then prophesy again. Some assume that John prophesied the remaining contents found in the book of Revelation (Rev. 11–22). Thus, the essence of what John saw was the Antichrist (Rev. 11–13) that Daniel prophesied about (Dan. 7–12).

C.   *Sweet:* speaks of the message of victory, salvation, justice, and deliverance for the oppressed

D.   *Bitter:* speaks of the message of judgment that also brings persecution to the messengers

IV.   THE TRIBULATION TEMPLE AND THE TRAMPLING OF JERUSALEM (REV. 11:1–2)

A.   The paradox in the tribulation temple is that it is God's temple, yet the Antichrist will use it. This temple is referred to as the "temple of God" (2 Thes. 2:3–4; Rev. 11:1).

> *[1]I was given a reed like a measuring rod. And the angel stood, saying, "Rise and measure the temple of God, the altar, and those who worship there. [2]But leave out the court which is outside the temple, and do not measure it, for it has been given to the Gentiles." (Rev. 11:1–2)*

1.   The tribulation temple will be built by unbelieving Jews and desecrated by the Antichrist in context to the abomination of desolation (Mt. 24:15; 2 Thes. 2:4; Rev. 11:1–2; 13:12–18; cf. Dan. 8:13; 9:27; 11:31, 36–37; 12:11). This temple is not the millennial temple.

> *[15]"When you see the 'abomination of desolation,' spoken of by Daniel the prophet, standing in the holy place…" (Mt. 24:15)*

> *[3]The son of perdition [Antichrist], [4]who…exalts himself above all that is called God… so that he sits as God in the temple of God, showing himself that he is God. (2 Thes. 2:3–4)*

2.   The millennial temple will be built by Jesus (Ezek. 37:26–28; 40–48; cf. Isa. 2:3; 60:13; Jer. 33:18; Joel 3:18; Mic. 4:2; Hab. 2:20; Hag. 2:7–9; Zech. 6:12–15; 14:16–21; Mal. 3:1–3).

B.   *Measure the temple:* John was told to measure the temple, altar, and its worshipers. To measure something spiritually means to evaluate it carefully and to discern its quality and purpose.

1.   Amos saw a plumb line in God's hand indicating that He "measured" Israel's obedience.

> *[8]The LORD said to me, "Amos, what do you see?" And I said, "A plumb line." Then the Lord said: "Behold, I am setting a plumb line in the midst of My people Israel…" (Amos 7:8)*

2.   During Belshazzar's royal feast in Babylon, a finger appeared and wrote on the wall that God had weighed or "measured" their kingdom and found it lacking (Dan. 5:27).

> *[26]This is the interpretation of each word. MENE: God has numbered your kingdom, and finished it; [27]TEKEL: You have been weighed in the balances, and found wanting. (Dan. 5:26–27)*

3.   We are to measure or carefully weight the issues related to God's purpose for the tribulation temple including what God-fearing Jews will do related to it in the end times. This will require insight from God into the various paradoxes and tensions related to it.

C.   God has a purpose for unbelieving yet God-fearing Jews being involved in various temple activities. We are not to dismiss all their activities in the temple as worthless. However, the only way of salvation for these God-fearing Jews is *through Jesus*, not through their temple activities.

D.	The temptation of some will be to criticize *all* the activities related to the tribulation temple, while the temptation of others will be to accept *all* these activities as being good and godly.

E.	The city of Jerusalem will be trampled by the Gentiles (Rev. 11:2).

²"Leave out the court which is outside the temple, and do not measure it, for it has been <u>given to the Gentiles</u>. And they will <u>tread the holy city underfoot</u> for forty-two months." (Rev. 11:2)

F.	***Tread the city underfoot:*** To be trodden under foot is symbolic of being conquered and crushed to the ground. Grapes were trodden under foot (Judges 9:27; Isa. 16:10; 63:2).

1.	Jesus prophesied that Jerusalem would be surrounded and trampled by Gentile armies. This was partially fulfilled in AD 70, and it will completely fulfilled in the end times.

²⁰"When you see <u>Jerusalem surrounded by armies</u>, then know that its desolation is near. ²¹Then let those who are in Judea flee to the mountains…²⁴They will fall by the edge of the sword, and be led away <u>captive</u> into all nations. And <u>Jerusalem will be trampled by Gentiles</u>." (Lk. 21:20–24)

¹⁵"Therefore when you see the 'abomination of desolation'…¹⁶then let those who are in Judea <u>flee to the mountains</u>…²¹For then there will be <u>great tribulation</u>, such as has not been since the beginning of the world until this time, no, nor ever shall be." (Mt. 24:15–21)

2.	The trampling of Jerusalem includes its siege and capture by the armies of the Antichrist.

²I will gather <u>all the nations to battle against Jerusalem</u>; the city shall be <u>taken</u>…Half of the city shall go into <u>captivity</u>… (Zech. 14:2)

²"…when they lay <u>siege</u> against Judah and Jerusalem…³<u>all nations</u> of the earth are gathered against it." (Zech. 12:2–3)

G.	***42 months:*** This is the same 3½ year time frame as *1,260 days* (Rev. 11:3; 12:6), *time, times, and half a time* (Rev. 12:14), and *42 months* (Rev. 13:5). There are eight scriptures and four phrases that describe the final 3½ years before Jesus returns—*1260 days* (Rev. 11:3; 12:6); *42 months* (Rev. 11:2; 13:5); *time, times and half a time* (Rev. 12:14; Dan. 7:25; 12:7); and the *middle of the week* (Dan. 9:27). Different terminology is used so that the meaning is clear and no one would easily be able to dismiss this significant prophetic time frame as symbolic.

H.	In Revelation 11, Jerusalem is called the *holy city* (v. 2), the *great city*, *Sodom,* and *Egypt* (v. 8).

²They will tread the <u>holy city</u> underfoot for forty-two months…⁸the <u>great city</u> which spiritually is called <u>Sodom</u> and <u>Egypt</u>, where also our Lord was crucified. (Rev. 11:2, 8)

1.	***Holy city:*** Jerusalem is the only city upon which the Lord placed His name and glory.

2.	***Great city:*** Jerusalem is great in its importance and prominence in God's plan.

3.	***Sodom:*** Jerusalem will be called Sodom because of the *perversion* that will occur there.

4.   *Egypt:* Jerusalem will be called Egypt because of the *oppression* that will occur there.

V.   THE TWO WITNESSES (REV. 11:3–6, 10)

A.   The two witnesses are powerful prophets who will release God's judgments on the Antichrist.

³"I will give power to my <u>two witnesses</u>, and they will <u>prophesy</u> one thousand two hundred and sixty days…" ⁵And if anyone wants to harm them, <u>fire</u> proceeds from their mouth and devours their enemies…⁶These have power to shut heaven, so that <u>no rain</u> falls in the days of their prophecy; and they have power over waters to turn them to <u>blood</u>, and to strike the earth with all plagues, as often as they desire. (Rev. 11:3–6)

B.   The two witnesses will release God's judgments on the Antichrist's empire in a way that will be similar to what Moses did on Pharaoh's empire. The plagues of Egypt are the prototype of the end-time judgments. The confrontation between Moses and the Pharaoh gives us insight into the confrontation between the two witnesses and the Antichrist. The miracles done by Elijah and Moses will be done by the two witnesses—miracles like these were referred to by the prophets (Mic. 7:15; cf. Isa. 10:22–25; 11:12–16; 30:30; Jer. 16:14–15; 23:7–8; Ezek. 38:22; Joel 2:30).

C.   Food was supernaturally provided in God's plan in the days of Moses, Elijah, and Jesus (who fed the 5,000). This may happen again as indicated in Revelation 12:13–17.

D.   The two witnesses will be killed and then raised from dead before all the nations (Rev. 11:7–10).

⁷When they finish their testimony, the beast [Antichrist]…will make war against them, overcome them, and <u>kill them</u>. ⁸And their dead bodies will lie in the street of the great city [Jerusalem] which spiritually is called Sodom and Egypt, where also our Lord was crucified. ⁹Then those from the peoples, tribes, tongues, and nations will <u>see</u> their dead bodies three-and-a-half days, and not allow their dead bodies to be put into graves. ¹⁰And those who dwell on the earth will rejoice over them, make merry, and send gifts to one another, because these two prophets tormented those who dwell on the earth. (Rev. 11:7–10)

E.   The nations will rejoice at their death to the degree they rage against Jesus' taking them over. They will see the two witnesses as those who tormented them.

¹¹Now after the three-and-a-half days the breath of life from God entered them, and they stood on their feet, and great fear fell on those who saw them. ¹²And they heard a loud voice from heaven saying to them, "Come up here." And they <u>ascended to heaven in a cloud</u>, and their enemies saw them. ¹³In the same hour there was a <u>great earthquake</u>, and a tenth of the city fell. In the earthquake seven thousand people were killed, and the rest were afraid and <u>gave glory</u> to the God of heaven. (Rev. 11:11–13)

Session 9: Second Coming and Rapture—War in the Spirit (Rev. 11–14)

I. THE RAPTURE AND REPLACEMENT OF WORLD GOVERNMENTS (REV. 11:15–19)

A. This is the third chronological section in which events in Jesus' end-time action plan are seen. At the seventh trumpet, an announcement in heaven will declare that the Lord will take over and replace all the governments on earth. At this time, He will also do three things—He will judge the dead, reward the saints, and destroy the leaders who are responsible for destroying the earth.

> [15] *Then the <u>seventh angel sounded</u>: And there were loud voices in heaven, saying, "<u>The kingdoms of this world have become the kingdoms of our Lord</u> and of His Christ, and He shall reign forever and ever!"* [16] *And the twenty-four elders…worshiped God,* [17] *saying: "We give You thanks… because You have taken Your great power and reigned.* [18] *The nations were angry, and Your wrath has come, and the time of the <u>dead</u>, that <u>they should be judged</u>, and that You should <u>reward Your servants</u>…and should <u>destroy those who destroy the earth</u>." (Rev. 11:15–18)*

1. Paul prophesied that the rapture will occur at the seventh trumpet (1 Cor. 15:51–52).

   > [51] *Behold, I tell you a <u>mystery</u>: We shall not all sleep, but we shall all be changed—* [52] *in a moment, in the twinkling of an eye, at the <u>last trumpet</u>. For the trumpet will sound, and the dead will be raised incorruptible, and we shall be changed. (1 Cor. 15:51–52)*

   > [7] *…in the days of the <u>sounding of the seventh angel</u>, when he is about to sound, the <u>mystery of God would be finished</u>, as He declared to His…prophets. (Rev. 10:7)*

2. The saints who are alive at the time of Jesus' coming will be raptured (1 Thes. 4:16–17).

   > [16] *The Lord Himself will descend from heaven…with the <u>trumpet of God</u>…* [17] *We who are alive…shall be <u>caught up</u> [raptured] together with them in the clouds to meet the Lord in the air. (1 Thes. 4:16–17)*

II. THIRD ANGELIC EXPLANATION (PARENTHESIS): WAR IN THE SPIRIT (REV. 12–14)

A. The third angelic explanation is a parenthetical section (Rev. 12–14). There will be a fierce war in the spirit between Satan and God's people leading up to the rapture. This section answers why God's wrath is so severe and requires replacing all the governments on earth. Satan and the Antichrist will violently attack God's people (Rev. 12–13). Jesus will help the saints (Rev. 14).

1. Revelation 12 describes war in the heavens between Satan and Michael the archangel.

2. Revelation 13 describes war on the earth between the Antichrist and the saints.

3. Revelation 14 describes seven visions that give insight into the different ways in which the Lord will intervene to empower the Church to walk in great victory.

B.   The seven main symbols in the book of Revelation are in this parenthetical section (Rev. 12–14). Daniel used most of these symbols (Dan 7:3–7, 12, 17; 8:4). He described the Antichrist as the Beast with a vast empire (Dan. 7:7, 11, 19–23) supported by ten kings whom he described as the ten horns on the Antichrist (Dan. 7:7, 20, 24; 2:41–42; Rev. 12:3; 13:1; 17:3, 7, 12, 16).

C.   *The dragon*: is always symbolic of Satan (Rev. 12:3, 4, 7, 9, 13, 16, 17; 13:2, 4; 16:13; 20:2)

D.   *The first Beast*: is symbolic of the Antichrist (Rev. 13; 14:9–11; 17:3–17; 19:19–21; 20:4, 10)

E.   *Another Beast*: is symbolic of the False Prophet who is only called "another Beast" one time. Every other time he is called the False Prophet (Rev. 13:11–17; 16:13; 19:20; 20:10).

F.   *The 7 heads*: the seven empires that persecute Israel are Egypt, Assyria, Babylon, Persia, Greece, Rome, and the revived Roman Empire (Dan. 2:41–42; 7:7, 20, 24; Rev. 12:3; 13:1; 17:3–16).

G.   *The 10 horns*: speaks of a future 10-nation confederation of ten kings who rule simultaneously over their own nation while coming into enthusiastic agreement or partnership together under the Antichrist's authority (Dan. 2:41–42; 7:7, 20, 24; 11:36–45; Rev. 12:3; 13:1; 17:3, 7, 12, 16)

H.   *The Harlot Babylon*: includes the literal re-built city of Babylon on the Euphrates River in Iraq (50 miles south of Baghdad) that will be restored and used as a headquarters for the Antichrist. It will function as a center of worldwide demonic religious and economic networks (Rev. 17–18; cf. Isa. 13–14; 21; Jer. 50–51), and will seduce many to sin while also persecuting the saints.

I.   *The Woman with the Male-child (Jesus)*: The woman is the faithful remnant of Israel through history (Rev. 12:1–5). Satan wars with her offspring who are Gentile believers (Rev. 12:17).

III. WAR BREAKS OUT IN HEAVEN (REV. 12)

A.   War will break out in heaven between Satan and Michael the archangel (Rev. 12:7–12). The result is that Satan will be cast to the earth at the beginning of the Great Tribulation.

   ⁷War broke out in heaven: Michael and his angels fought with the dragon [Satan]; and the dragon and his angels fought, ⁸but they did not prevail, nor was a place found for them in heaven any longer. ⁹The great dragon…called the Devil…was cast to the earth, and his angels were cast out with him…¹²"Woe to the inhabitants of the earth…For the devil has come down to you, having great wrath [fury, NIV], because he knows that he has a short time." (Rev. 12:7–12)

B.   Some teach that this war in heaven occurred at the cross and that Satan is now confined to the earth. However, we war against Satan's host operating in the heavenly places in this age.

   ¹²We do not wrestle against flesh and blood, but against principalities…against the rulers of the darkness…against spiritual hosts of wickedness in the heavenly places. (Eph. 6:12)

C.   One of unique dynamics in the end times is that Satan and all his demons will be cast to the earth (Rev. 12:9). He will give his throne to the Antichrist (Rev. 13:2). Multitudes of demons now in the bottomless pit will be released onto the earth (Rev. 9:3, 16).

   ²The dragon [Satan] gave him [Antichrist] his power, his throne … (Rev. 13:2)

IV. THE END-TIME PERSECUTION OF SATAN AGAINST GOD'S PEOPLE (REV. 12:13–17)

[13]Now when the dragon [Satan] saw that he had been cast to the earth, he persecuted the woman [remnant of Israel] who gave birth to the male Child [Jesus]. [14]But the woman was given two wings of a great eagle, <u>that she might fly into the wilderness</u> to her place, where she is <u>nourished</u> for a time and times and half a time [3½ years], from the presence of the serpent [Satan]. [15]So the serpent spewed water out of his mouth [persecution] like a flood after the woman, that he might cause her to be carried away by the flood [destroyed]. [16]But the earth [natural elements touched by God's power] helped the woman, and the earth opened its mouth and swallowed up the flood which the dragon had spewed out of his mouth. [17]And the dragon was enraged with the woman, and <u>he went to make war with the rest of her offspring</u> [end-time Church], who keep the commandments of God and have the testimony of Jesus Christ. (Rev. 12:13–17).

A. When Satan sees he is confined to earth, he will persecute Israel and the saints (Rev. 12:13, 17).

B. The woman or remnant of Israel is given two wings of a great eagle. This speaks of at time when God will miraculously deliver, protect, and provide for her in the wilderness. God manifested the strength, swiftness, and attentiveness of an eagle to care for Israel in the time of the Exodus from Egypt. He continued His care for the next forty years, providing manna from the sky and water from a rock. He protected them from the hostility of neighboring nations.

[4]"You have seen what I did to the Egyptians, and how I bore you on <u>eagles' wings</u>.'" (Ex. 19:4)

[11]"<u>As an eagle</u> stirs up its nest, hovers over its young, spreading out its wings, taking them up, <u>carrying</u> them on its wings, [12]<u>so the LORD alone led him</u>…" (Deut. 32:11–12)

C. Israel will flee into the wilderness to *her place* where she is *nourished* and protected from the presence of Satan for 3½ years (Rev. 12:14). Satan will seek to destroy all Israel (Rev. 12:15).

V. SATAN WARS THROUGH THE ANTICHRIST AND FALSE PROPHET (REV. 13)

A. Satan will seek to destroy Israel and the Church (Rev. 12:17). In Revelation 13, Satan will give his authority to the Antichrist to complete his plan to destroy Israel and the Church (Rev. 13:2). Revelation 13 describes the resources that the Antichrist will have to war against God's people.

B. The Antichrist will be a world leader who has a political, military, and economic alliance with ten nations, giving him the largest empire and the most powerful army in history. The Antichrist will be fully human, yet fully demonized with Satan's authority (Rev. 13:2).

[2]The dragon [Satan] gave him [Antichrist] his <u>power</u>, his <u>throne</u>, and <u>great authority</u>…[4]They worshiped the dragon…and they worshiped the beast, saying, "Who is like the beast? Who is able to make war with him?"… [7]It was granted to him [Antichrist] <u>to make war with the saints</u> and to overcome [kill] them. <u>And authority was given him</u> over every tribe…and nation. (Rev. 13:2–7)

C. The Antichrist will claim to be God and will demand that the whole earth worship him as he seeks to assert his authority over the nations. He will have authority and worshippers in all nations, *yet will not totally dominate them all.* There will be nations who resist him (Dan. 11:40–45; Rev. 16:14).

D.   The Antichrist will seek to kill anyone who refuses to worship him (Rev. 13:8, 12, 15). This will lead billions of people to engage in Satan worship.

> *8All who dwell on the earth will worship him [Antichrist], whose names have not been written in the Book of Life of the Lamb slain from the foundation of the world. (Rev. 13:8)*

E.   The False Prophet will be the leader of a future worldwide religious network that will be devoted to causing all the nations to worship the Antichrist (Rev. 13:11–18).

> *11I saw another beast [False Prophet]…he had two horns like a lamb and spoke like a dragon. (Rev. 13:11)*

F.   John highlighted three strategies the False Prophet will use to get the nations to worship the Beast.

G.   First, he will be a prophet with a message. His demonically empowered *public speeches* will be confirmed by great miracles that will deceive the masses (Rev. 13:12–14).

> *12He exercises all the authority of the first beast…and causes the earth and those who dwell in it to worship the first beast…13He performs great signs…14He deceives those who dwell on the earth by those signs… (Rev. 13:12–14)*

H.   Second, he will establish a worship system related to the abomination of desolation (Mt. 24:15; 2 Thes. 2:3–4). An image or stature of the Antichrist will be set up in the temple. It will be a demonically empowered statue that appears to breath and speak (Rev. 13:14–15).

> *14Telling those who dwell on earth to make an image [statue] to the beast…15He was granted power to give breath to the image of the beast, that the image of the beast should both speak and cause as many as would not worship the image of the beast to be killed. (Rev. 13:14–15)*

1.   The abomination of desolation will be a series of abominable or evil events. They will be an abomination to God that results in global desolation or destruction. The abomination will be the Antichrist's claim to be God, along with his demand that all worship him.

> *15"When you see the 'abomination of desolation,' spoken of by Daniel the prophet, standing in the holy place…16then let those who are in Judea flee to the mountains." (Mt. 24:15–16)*

> *3The son of perdition [Antichrist] 4who opposes and exalts himself above all that is called God…sits as God in the temple of God, showing himself that he is God. (2 Thes. 2:3–4)*

2.   The image of the Beast may combine cutting-edge technology and demonic elements that cause the image to appear to breathe and speak. The image may be a high-tech hologram that looks and sounds like the Antichrist. Some suggest that there may be many regional Antichrist worship centers with a duplicate image of the Antichrist that is connected to the "primary" image in Jerusalem by technology, the result being a global network of local "Antichrist worship sanctuaries" that may each include a hologram of the Antichrist.

3.   The law will require all to worship the Antichrist (Rev. 13:12, 15). Those who refuse will be guilty of the death penalty. He will use the power of the state to kill all who resist him.

I.   Third, he will establish a worldwide economic system that forces the nations to worship the Antichrist by the *mark of the Beast* put on their hand or forehead to force everyone to declare publicly their loyalty to the Antichrist. Those refusing this mark will not be able to buy or sell.

> *[16]He causes all…to receive a mark on their right hand or on their foreheads, [17]and that no one may buy or sell except one who has the mark…[18]His number is 666. (Rev. 13:16–18)*

VI.   JESUS WILL SUPERNATURALLY HELP THE CHURCH COME TO VICTORY (REV. 14)

A.   The purpose of this part of this parenthetical section is to give insight into the certainty of victory for the saints and to give understanding regarding why God's wrath is so severe in replacing all the governments of the earth in the seventh trumpet (Rev. 11:15).

B.   God promised to intervene to help the saints (Rev. 14:1–20). Note three sections in this chapter. In the first section, the 144,000 first fruits of Israel will be a model of victory for others (Rev. 14:1–5). In the second section, we see four proclamations that the Spirit will anoint (Rev. 14:6–13). In the third section, we see a two-fold harvest of salvation and judgment (Rev. 14:14–20).

VII. FIRST SECTION: THE 144,000 FIRST FRUITS OF ISRAEL (REV. 14:1–5)

A.   John saw Jesus standing on Mount Zion in Jerusalem with 144,000 singers (Rev. 14:1–5). These 144,000 singers will be a model of victory in the midst of persecution as they provide great strength to the Church by their prophetic singing that releases God's power. These singers will prophesy with power. They will be sealed or protected from judgment (Rev. 7:4–8).

> *[1]Behold, a <u>Lamb standing on Mount Zion</u>, and with Him 144,000, having His Father's name written on their foreheads. [2]And I heard a voice from heaven, like the voice of many waters, and like the voice of loud thunder. And I heard the sound of harpists playing their harps. [3]They [the harpists] sang as it were a new song before the throne…and <u>no one could learn that song except the 144,000</u>…[4]These are the ones who were <u>not defiled</u> with [immoral] women, for they are <u>virgins</u> [celibates]. These are the ones who <u>follow the Lamb</u> wherever He goes…[5]In their mouth was found <u>no deceit</u>, for they are <u>without fault</u> [compromise]… (Rev. 14:1–5)*

B.   They will be deeply dedicated to Jesus as seen by the five virtues stated in verses 4–5.

VIII. SECOND SECTION: FOUR PROCLAMATIONS THE SPIRIT WILL ANOINT (REV. 14:6–13)

A.   John identified four promises or messages that must be boldly proclaimed (Rev. 14:6–13). I believe that the Spirit will release power to confirm these messages to strengthen His people.

B.   ***The message of the certainty of gospel being preached in all nations*** (Rev. 14:6–7): There will be angelic assistance and power to succeed in preaching the Gospel to all nations in the presence of great hostility (Mt. 24:14; Rev. 7:9).

> *[6]I saw another angel flying in the midst of heaven, having the <u>everlasting gospel to preach</u> to those who dwell on the earth—to every nation, tribe, tongue, and people—[7]saying with a loud voice, "<u>Fear God</u> and <u>give glory to Him</u>, for the hour of <u>His judgment</u> has come; and worship Him who made heaven and earth, the sea and springs of water." (Rev. 14:6–7)*

C.   ***The message of the certainty of the judgment on Harlot Babylon*** (Rev. 14:8): The proclamation of the message of the total defeat of the Harlot Babylon will strengthen the Church (Rev. 17–18).

> *⁸Another angel followed, saying, "<u>Babylon is fallen</u>, is fallen, that great city, because she has made all nations drink of the wine of the wrath of her fornication." (Rev. 14:8)*

D.   ***The message of the certainty of eternal judgment*** (Rev. 14:9–11): This message is for those who accept the mark of the Beast. There will be an anointed proclamation of the certainty of eternal judgment coming on all who worship the Antichrist. Confidence that the Antichrist will surely be judged will embolden the saints to resist his deceptive allurements and terrifying threats.

> *⁹Then a third angel followed them, saying with a loud voice, "If anyone worships the beast… ¹⁰he himself shall also drink of the wine of the <u>wrath of God</u>, which is poured out full strength into the cup of His indignation. He shall be tormented with fire and brimstone… ¹¹The smoke of their torment ascends forever and ever; and they have no rest day or night, who worship the beast…and whoever receives the mark of his name." (Rev. 14:9–11)*

E.   ***The message of eternal rewards for faithfulness (Rev. 14:13)***: This will strengthen His people.

> *¹²Here is the patience [perseverance] of the saints; here are those who keep the commandments of God and the faith of Jesus. ¹³Then I heard a voice from heaven saying to me, "Write: 'Blessed are the dead who die in the Lord from now on.'" "Yes," says the Spirit, "that they may rest from their labors, and their works follow them." (Rev. 14:12–13)*

IX.   THIRD SECTION: HARVEST OF SALVATION AND JUDGMENT (REV. 14:14–20)

A.   John saw two end-time harvests: of souls (Rev. 14:14–16) and of judgment (Rev. 14:17–20).

> *¹⁴Behold…One like the Son of Man [Jesus], having on His head a golden crown, and in His hand a sharp sickle. ¹⁵And another angel came out of the temple, crying with a loud voice to Him… "Thrust in Your sickle and reap…for the harvest of the earth is ripe." (Rev. 14:14–15)*

B.   All the kings of the earth will be gathered into one geographic area (Zech. 12:2–3; 14:2; cf. Joel 3:2, 12; Zeph. 3:8; Rev. 16:14). Jesus will kill them in "this winepress" (Rev. 19:19–21). A winepress was associated with the celebration of the harvest.

C.   The harvest of judgment will result in a river of blood will run nearly 200 miles or the distance from Megiddo in the north to Bozrah in the south (Israel is 160 miles from north to south). Isaiah saw the Messiah marching to Jerusalem from Jordan (Bozrah in Edom) in the south (Isa. 63:1–6).

> *¹⁷Another angel came…having a sharp sickle. ¹⁸And another angel came out from the altar…cried with a loud cry to him who had the sharp sickle, saying, "Thrust in your sharp sickle and gather the clusters of the vine of the earth, <u>for her grapes are fully ripe</u>." ¹⁹So the angel thrust his sickle into the earth and <u>gathered the vine of the earth</u>, and threw it into the great winepress of the <u>wrath of God</u>. ²⁰And the winepress was trampled…and blood came out of the winepress, up to the horses' bridles, for 1,600 furlongs [200 miles]. (Rev. 14:17–20)*

Session 10: Seven Bowls of Wrath (Rev. 15–16)

I. INTRODUCTION TO THE SEVEN BOWLS OF WRATH (REV. 15:1–16:21)

A. The fourth chronological section of the book of Revelation describes the seven bowl judgment events that Jesus will release upon the Antichrist's empire. I see the events in this section as occurring right after the sounding of the seventh trumpet in which an announcement in heaven declares that the Lord is taking over and replacing all the governments on earth (Rev. 11:15).

[15]Then the <u>seventh angel sounded</u>: And there were loud voices in heaven, saying, "<u>The kingdoms of this world have become the kingdoms of our Lord</u>…and He shall reign forever and ever!" (Rev. 11:15)

B. Paul prophesied that the rapture would occur at the last trumpet (1 Cor. 15:51–52). These seven trumpets in the book of Revelation are the *only* trumpets that are numbered in the Bible (Rev. 8–9). I believe that Paul's "last" trumpet is the seventh trumpet mentioned in Revelation 10:7, 11:15, since it is the "last" trumpet mentioned in Revelation. If the rapture does not occur at the seventh trumpet, then it must occur sometime *after* it to occur at the "last" trumpet. The last trumpet by definition cannot be *before* the seventh trumpet (or any other trumpet)—it is the *very last* to sound in this age.

[51]Behold, I tell you a <u>mystery</u>: We shall not all sleep, but we shall all be <u>changed</u>—[52]in a moment, in the twinkling of an eye, at the <u>last trumpet</u>. For the trumpet will sound, and the dead will be raised incorruptible, and we shall be <u>changed</u> [the rapture]. (1 Cor. 15:51–52)

C. Daniel prophesied that the abomination of desolation would continue for *1,290 days* (43 months).

[11]"And from the time that the daily sacrifice is taken away, and the abomination of desolation is <u>set up</u>, there shall be <u>one thousand two hundred and ninety days</u> [1290 days]." (Dan. 12:11)

1. The Antichrist will set up the abomination of desolation after he stops the sacrifices in the Jerusalem temple, which will be rebuilt. He will put an image of himself in the holy place and require people to worship him as God (Mt. 24:15; 2 Thes. 2:4; Rev. 13:14–18).

[15]"When you <u>see</u> the 'abomination of desolation' spoken of by Daniel the prophet, standing in the holy place…[16]then let those who are in Judea flee to the mountains." (Mt. 24:15–16)

2. *For more on the abomination of desolation see the *additional study materials*, page 5ff.

D. Daniel emphasized a *1,290-day* (43 month) period that begins on the day the abomination is set up; however John only addressed a *1,260-day* (42 month) period that also begins at that time. John highlighted three activities that will continue for exactly 1,260 days (42 months). Notice that John's 1,260 days (42 months) are 30 days *short* of Daniel's time period (Dan. 12:11).

1. *Provision*: God will supernaturally provide for Israel for exactly 1,260 days (Rev. 12:6, 14).

2. *Prophecy*: The two witnesses will prophesy for exactly 1,260 days (Rev. 11:3).

3. *Persecution*: The Antichrist will war against the saints (Dan. 7:25; Rev. 13:5–7) and dominate Jerusalem (Rev. 11:2; Dan. 12:7) for exactly 1,260 days.

E.   The Antichrist's activities will *continue for an additional 30 days* after Israel's provision in the wilderness (Rev. 12:6), the prophesying of the two witnesses (Rev. 11:3), and the persecution of the saints and Jerusalem (Rev. 11:2) are over. This coincides with the sounding of the seventh trumpet.

F.   In other words, on the 1,260th day (42nd month or 3½ years) after the abomination of desolation begins, I believe that the seventh trumpet will sound, the Church will be raptured (Rev. 11:15), and the Antichrist's *unchallenged* domination of Jerusalem will come to an end. His focus will then change in a dramatic way during the final 30 days (the 43rd month) as He stops persecuting Israel and the Church to rally the nations to make war against Jesus (Rev. 17:14; 19:11, 19).

G.   There will be three types of people on earth when Jesus appears in the sky:

1.   The *redeemed* will be raptured during Jesus' worldwide procession across the sky.

2.   The *reprobate*, who took the mark of the Beast, will be killed (some executed).

3.   The *resisters* are the unsaved survivors of the Great Tribulation, who will refuse to worship the Antichrist, even though they were not saved. Scripture refers to them as *those left* or *those who remain* (Isa. 4:3; 10:20; 11:11; 49:6; 65:8; 66:19; Jer. 31:2; Ezek. 20:38–42; 36:36; Dan. 12:1; Amos 9:9–10; Joel 2:32; Zech. 12:14; 13:8; 14:16). These will have an opportunity to be saved after Jesus returns to earth and will populate the millennial earth.

II.   JESUS' ROYAL PROCESSION: THREE STAGES

A.   At the seventh trumpet, I believe that Jesus will rapture the Church and make His royal procession across the earth. In my opinion, His coming with all the saints involves *a royal procession* that has three stages, which will include many events occurring over a 30-day period.

Stage 1: Jesus' procession *across the sky* to rapture the Church (Mt. 24:30–31; Rev. 1:7)
Stage 2: Jesus' procession *on the land* marching through Edom (Jordan) to Israel (Isa. 63)
Stage 3: Jesus' procession *into Jerusalem* from the Mount of Olives, followed by His coronation

B.   *Stage 1*: Every person will see Jesus' royal procession *across the sky* (Rev. 1:7) just before He raptures the Church (Mt. 24:30–31). With trumpets, His kingship will be announced over each nation. His coming to gather His elect will not be a secret coming, but one that is seen by everyone.

⁷Behold, He is coming with clouds, and every eye will see Him, even they who pierced Him. And all the tribes of the earth will mourn because of Him. (Rev. 1:7)

²⁹"Immediately after the tribulation of those days the sun will be darkened…³⁰Then the sign of the Son of Man will appear in heaven, and then all the tribes of the earth will mourn, and they will see the Son of Man coming on the clouds of heaven with power and great glory. ³¹And He will send His angels with a great sound of a trumpet, and they will gather [rapture] together His elect [saints] from the four winds, from one end of heaven to the other." (Mt 24:29–31)

1.   *The sign*: In my opinion, the sign of the Son of Man may be related to His royal procession around the whole earth. Jesus will come with all the angels and saints from heaven (Mt. 25:31; 1 Thes. 3:13) as He travels on clouds in the Father's glory (Mt. 16:27), great power (Mk. 13:26), and flaming fire (2 Thes. 1:8). He will descend with a great shout, the voice of an archangel, and with the trumpet of God as He raises the dead (1 Thes. 4:14–16).

2. *Mourn*: Every unbeliever will see Him clearly enough to have a deep emotional response described as mourning. Thus, Jesus will travel close enough to the earth and slowly enough across the face of the earth for *every unbeliever* to see Him clearly enough to understand what is happening so that they mourn over having not received Him before this time.

C. *Stage 2*: Jesus' royal procession *on the land* as He travels through Edom (modern-day Jordan) on His way to Jerusalem with great victory over the armies of the Antichrist (Isa. 63:1–6; cf. Ps. 45:3–5; 110:5–6; Hab. 3:12; Rev. 19:19). Jesus will march to Jerusalem as the "greater Moses." In my opinion, He will release the bowl judgments on the Antichrist, of whom Pharaoh was a type. Jesus will liberate Jerusalem and kill the Antichrist's armies, ending the abomination of desolation.

[1]Who is this who comes from Edom [modern Jordan], with dyed garments from Bozrah [ancient capital of Edom], this One [Jesus] who is glorious in His apparel, traveling in the greatness of His strength?—"I [Jesus] who speak in righteousness, mighty to save." [2]Why is Your apparel red, and Your garments like one who treads in the winepress? [3]"I have trodden the winepress…in My anger, and trampled them in My fury; their blood is sprinkled upon My garments, and I have stained all My robes. [4]For the day of vengeance is in My heart, and the year of My redeemed has come." (Isa. 63:1–4)

D. *Stage 3*: Jesus' triumphal entry *into Jerusalem* from the Mount of Olives (Zechariah 14:4), received by the leaders of Jerusalem, followed by His coronation as King (Ps. 24:7–10; Zech. 14:1–5; Mt. 23:39)

[39]"…you shall see Me no more till you say, 'Blessed is He who comes in the name of the LORD!'" (Mt 23:39)

[7]Lift up your heads, O you gates! And be lifted up, you everlasting doors! And the King of glory shall come in. [8]Who is this King of glory? The LORD strong and mighty…mighty in battle. (Ps. 24:7–8)

III. THE HEAVENLY CONTEXT TO RELEASE THE BOWLS OF WRATH (REV. 15)

A. John saw end-time believers, who were victorious over the Antichrist, standing on the sea of glass in heaven singing about the glory of God (Rev. 15:1–4). This might describe the martyred saints who are already in heaven singing as they join the Lord as He raptures the Church.

[1]Then I saw another sign in heaven, great and marvelous: seven angels having the seven last plagues, for in them the wrath of God is complete. [2]And I saw something like a sea of glass mingled with fire, and those who have the victory over the beast [Antichrist]…standing on the sea of glass… [3]They sing the song of Moses…and the song of the Lamb, saying: "Great and marvelous are Your works, Lord God Almighty! Just and true are Your ways, O King of the saints… [4]For all nations shall…worship before You, for Your judgments have been manifested." (Rev. 15:1–4)

B. The temple opened in heaven, and seven angels received seven bowls of wrath (Rev. 15:5–8).

[5]After these things…the temple of the tabernacle of the testimony in heaven was opened. [6]And out of the temple came the seven angels having the seven plagues, clothed in pure bright linen, and having their chests girded with golden bands. [7]Then one of the four living creatures gave to the seven angels seven golden bowls full of the wrath of God who lives forever and ever.

⁸The temple was filled with smoke from the glory of God and from His power, and no one was able to enter the temple till the seven plagues of the seven angels were completed. (Rev. 15:5–8)

IV.   THE SEVEN BOWLS OF GOD'S WRATH (REV. 16)

A.   In the days of the sounding of the seventh trumpet, the saints in heaven gather on the sea of glass to worship the Lord and to participate in the rapture as the seven angels receive the bowls of wrath.

¹Then I heard a loud voice from the temple saying to the seven angels, "Go and pour out the bowls of the wrath of God on the earth." (Rev. 16:1)

B.   *First bowl (sores)*: sores will cause great suffering for those who worship the Antichrist (Rev. 16:2).

²So the first went and poured out his bowl…and a foul and loathsome sore came upon the men who had the mark of the beast [Antichrist]… (Rev. 16:2)

C.   *Second bowl (food supply)*: The sea will become blood, killing all the sea life (Rev. 16:3). This will be *complete* destruction of marine life, not just 1/3 destruction as in the second trumpet. The sea will become like the congealed blood of a dead man, with unimaginable stench. Some believe this refers only to the Mediterranean Sea since that is the context of Daniel 7.

³Then the second angel poured out his bowl on the sea, and it became blood as of a dead man; and every living creature in the sea died. (Rev. 16:3)

D.   *Third bowl (water supply)*: The earth's fresh water will be poisoned with blood (Rev. 16:4–7). The third trumpet (Rev. 8:10) is similar to the third bowl in defiling the drinking water. The first plague of Egypt struck the Nile with a similar impact as this (Ex. 7:19–21).

⁴Then the third angel poured out his bowl on the rivers and springs of water, and they became blood. ⁵And I heard the angel of the waters saying: "You are righteous, O Lord…because You have judged these things. ⁶For they have shed the blood of saints and prophets, and You have given them blood to drink. For it is their just due." ⁷And I heard another from the altar [heavenly intercession] saying, "Even so, Lord God Almighty, true and righteous are Your judgments." (Rev. 16:4–7)

E.   *Fourth bowl (torment)*: There will be scorching heat from the sun (Rev. 16:8–9). I see this as a supernatural act of God, not merely a natural one. This bowl will intensify the heat of the sun. The fourth trumpet affected the sun in the opposite way by making it less intense.

⁸Then the fourth angel poured out his bowl on the sun, and power was given to him to scorch men with fire. ⁹And men were scorched with great heat, and they blasphemed the name of God who has power over these plagues; and they did not repent and give Him glory. (Rev. 16:8–9)

F.   *Fifth bowl (darkness)*: Darkness will fall on the Antichrist's global empire (Rev. 16:10–11). This darkness will probably have a supernatural, demonic element to it. The ninth plague of Egypt caused darkness for three days (Ex. 10:21–23).

¹⁰Then the fifth angel poured out his bowl on the throne of the beast, and his kingdom became full of darkness; and they gnawed their tongues because of the pain. ¹¹They blasphemed the God of heaven because of their pains and their sores, and did not repent of their deeds. (Rev. 16:10–11)

G.   The Antichrist's worshipers will not repent, but will blaspheme God (Rev. 16:9, 11, 21), showing their deep hatred of Him. As God's judgments increase, the hatred and blasphemy of the wicked will come fully into the open.

V.   SIXTH BOWL: DEMONS LURE THE NATIONS TO ARMAGEDDON

A.   *Sixth bowl (global guilt)*: demons will lure the nations to gather to fight Jesus (Rev. 16:12–16).

[12]Then the sixth angel poured out his bowl on the river Euphrates, and its water was dried up, so that the way of the kings from the east might be prepared. [13]And I saw three unclean spirits like frogs coming out of the mouth of the dragon [Satan], out of the mouth of the beast [Antichrist], and out of the mouth of the false prophet. [14]For they are spirits of demons, performing signs, which go out to the kings of the earth…to gather them to the battle of that great day of God Almighty… [16]They gathered them together to…Armageddon. (Rev. 16:12–16)

B.   It is very surprising to me that the nations will come to fight Jesus as He marches toward Jerusalem. They are not gathering from around the world to fight Israel's small, poorly armed army.

[14]"These [the 10 kings] will make war with the Lamb, and the Lamb will overcome them, for He is…King of kings…" (Rev. 17:14)

[19]I saw the beast [Antichrist], the kings of the earth, and their armies, gathered together to make war against Him who sat on the horse and against His army. (Rev. 19:19)

C.   In my opinion, the kings of the nations will have urgency to gather because of Jesus' sign in the sky. The Antichrist will convince the kings of the earth that defeating Jesus is necessary and doable. The kings will see the sign of the Son of Man in the sky (Mt. 24:30), but wrongly interpret it as a demonic sign of a false messiah coming to disrupt the kingdoms of the earth.

[30]"Then the sign of the Son of Man will appear in heaven…all the tribes of the earth will mourn…they will see the Son of Man coming on the clouds…with power and great glory." (Mt. 24:30)

D.   In the Antichrist's final 30 days, he will use his greatest miracles to win the kings who had been resisting him. Why would the Antichrist prioritize mobilizing the nations to come to Israel for military reasons? Why would the kings of the east deploy hundreds of thousands of soldiers (costing untold billions of dollars) to fight a weak Israeli army in Jerusalem?

E.   The Pharisees accused Jesus of doing miracles by Satan's power (Mt. 12:24). Jesus taught that to attribute the power of the Spirit to Satan is to blaspheme against the Spirit. Only people who are hardened to such a degree that they will not repent do this.

[31]"Every sin and blasphemy will be forgiven men, but the blasphemy against the Spirit will not be forgiven men. [32]Anyone who speaks a word against the Son of Man, it will be forgiven him; but whoever speaks against the Holy Spirit, it will not be forgiven him…" (Mt. 12:31–32)

F.   Blasphemy against the Spirit is a full and final rejection of the ministry of the Holy Spirit. Those who do this are reprobate or have a heart that is permanently hardened without any inclination to repent. The greatest height of evil is for men to blaspheme the Holy Spirit (Mt. 12:31–32).

G.   I see the sixth bowl as global blasphemy against the Spirit as the nations receive *"the lie"* (2 Thes. 2:10). I believe that this "lie" will include acknowledging Jesus' power as being demonic.

⁹The coming of the lawless one [Antichrist]…with all power, signs, and <u>lying wonders</u>, ¹⁰and with all unrighteous deception…because they did not receive the <u>love of the truth</u>…¹¹For this reason God will send them <u>strong delusion</u>, that they should believe <u>the lie</u>… (2 Thes. 2:9–11)

VI. SEVENTH BOWL: EARTHQUAKES AND HAIL STONES

A.   *Seventh bowl (annihilation)*: shaking by earthquakes and 100 lb. hail stones (Rev. 16:17–21)

¹⁷…poured out his bowl into the <u>air</u>, and a loud voice…from the throne, saying, "It is done!" ¹⁸…there was a <u>great earthquake</u>, such a mighty and great earthquake as had not occurred since men were on the earth. ¹⁹Now the great city [Jerusalem] was divided into three parts, and the cities of the nations fell. <u>And great Babylon</u> was remembered before God, to give her the cup of the wine of the fierceness of His wrath. ²⁰Then <u>every island fled away</u>, and the <u>mountains were not found</u>. ²¹And <u>great hail</u> from heaven fell upon men, each hailstone about the weight of a talent [100 pounds]. Men blasphemed God… (Rev. 16:17–21)

B.   This bowl poured out *into the air* is probably the cause of the plague Zechariah prophesied would make the flesh, eyes, and tongues of people and livestock dissolve (Zech. 14:12, 15).

C.   This bowl releases the worst earthquake in history that shakes the cities of the nations. In Rev. 16:20, the last earthquake causes islands to flee (sink in the ocean) and the mountains to fall. The earthquake will impact every city on earth as great skyscrapers collapse, causing fires. The earthquake sequence in Revelation (Rev. 6:14; 8:5; 11:13; 16:18–20) ends with the largest one (Isa. 2:10, 19, 21; 13:13; 29:6; Ezek. 38:19; Hag. 2:6, 21; Zech. 14:4–5; Heb. 12:26–27).

D.   The seventh bowl may be further described in Isaiah 24.

E.   Hailstones weighing 100 pounds (a talent) fall on the people seeking safety from earthquakes. A 100-pound hailstone hits the ground with the equivalent force of two tons. Hail was released in the first trumpet (Rev. 8:7) and the seventh plague with Moses (Ex. 9:23–24). God uses hail in His judgments (Josh. 10:11; Isa. 28:17; Ezek. 38:22–23).

²²"I will bring him [Antichrist] to judgment…I will rain down on…his troops, and on the many peoples who are with him, <u>flooding rain</u>, <u>great hailstones</u>, fire, and brimstone." (Ezek. 38:22)

F.   The law of Moses required the stoning to death of idol worshippers (Deut. 17:2–5; Lev. 24:16). Since the Antichrist's worship movement is idolatry, Jesus Himself will stone them to death from heaven.

G.   The next event after the seven bowls is Jesus' triumphal entry into Jerusalem (Rev. 19:11–21).

¹¹Behold, a white horse. And He [Jesus] who sat on him…judges and <u>makes war</u>…¹³He was clothed with a robe <u>dipped in blood</u>… ¹⁴The armies in heaven…followed Him on white horses…¹⁶He has on His robe…a name written: KING OF KINGS AND LORD OF LORDS…¹⁹I saw the beast, the kings of the earth, and <u>their armies</u>, gathered together to <u>make war against Him</u>…²⁰Then the beast was <u>captured</u>, and…cast alive into the lake of fire…²¹The rest were <u>killed</u> with the sword… (Rev. 19:11–21)

Session 11: The Fall of Babylon (Rev. 17–18)

I.   JOHN'S PROPHECY ABOUT THE FALL OF BABYLON (REV. 17–18)

A.   Revelation 17–18 is an angelic explanation (parenthetical section) that follows after the crisis described in the seven bowl judgments in Revelation 16.

B.   The five chronological sections in the book of Revelation tell us the main story line of God's judgment events against harlot Babylon and the Antichrist's empire. After each of the chronological sections, an angel explained to John why these judgment events are absolutely necessary. These explanations function as a parenthesis that puts the story line on "pause" as they answer questions as to *"Why is God's wrath so severe?"* and *"What will happen to the saints during the judgments?"*

C.   The seventh bowl will involve the most severe earthquake in history, followed by 100-pound hailstones that will destroy many cites of the earth (Rev. 16:17–21). The Antichrist's worshipers will not repent, but will stubbornly blaspheme God (Rev. 16:9, 11, 21).

[18]...there was a <u>great earthquake</u>, such a mighty and great earthquake as had not occurred since men were on the earth. [19]...<u>And great Babylon</u> was remembered before God, to give her the cup of the wine of the fierceness of His wrath...[21]And <u>great hail</u> from heaven fell upon men, each hailstone about the weight of a talent [100 pounds]. Men blasphemed God... (Rev. 16:18–21)

D.   In this angelic explanation, an angel showed John why it was necessary to destroy many cities of the earth and why Jesus will dash to pieces the societal infrastructure of the nations. It is because the seduction of Babylon's religion of evil will permeate so many of these structures of society. The seventh trumpet will focus on replacing evil leaders, and the seventh bowl will focus on replacing the social infrastructures (social, financial, and legal institutions that empowered evil activities).

[8]"'I will give You [Jesus] the nations for Your inheritance...[9]You shall <u>break them</u> with a rod of iron; You shall <u>dash them</u> to pieces like a potter's vessel.'" (Ps. 2:8–9)

E.   Revelation 17–18 is one of the most significant end-time prophecies because it gives us insight into Satan's strategy to deceive the nations while causing many Christians to fall away from the faith. This prophecy deserves careful study and dialogue because those who are deceived by the harlot will end up in the lake of fire, and many of the saints who resist the harlot will be killed (Rev. 17:6).

F.   The main message of Revelation 17 is easy to understand. The main themes are the seductive power and cruel persecution, along with the inevitable destruction of the harlot systems. Revelation 17 is the most symbolic passage in the book of Revelation, with many intricate details making it the most difficult chapter in Revelation to understand. Since the angel gave John the meaning of the symbols, we have a solid foundation for understanding this passage.

G.   In my opinion, the literal city of Babylon in Iraq (50 miles south of Baghdad) will be restored and used as one of the headquarters for the Antichrist and as a center of demonic religious and economic networks. As Jerusalem suddenly came out of the ashes and was rebuilt, I believe so also the city of Babylon in Iraq will suddenly be rebuilt. The judgments prophesied in Jeremiah 50–51 about the city of Babylon being suddenly and forever destroyed have not yet been fulfilled.

II.   THE END-TIME FALLING AWAY FROM THE FAITH

A.   The two signs that Paul gave to indicate the time of Jesus' coming are a falling away from the faith combined with the revealing of the Antichrist on the world stage (2 Thes. 2:3). Love of the truth is more than an intellectual adherence to truth; it takes a firm stand for truth regardless of the cost.

> *³Let no one deceive you by any means; for that Day [Jesus' second coming] will not come unless the falling away comes first, and the man of sin [Antichrist] is revealed…⁹The coming of the lawless one [Antichrist] is according to the working of Satan, with all power, signs, and lying wonders, ¹⁰and with all unrighteous deception among those who perish, because they did not receive the love of the truth, that they might be saved. (2 Thes. 2:3, 9–10)*

B.   There will be an end-time falling away (Mt. 24:9–13; 2 Thes. 2:3; 1 Tim. 4:1–2; 2 Tim. 3:1–7; 4:3–5; 2 Pet. 2:1–3). A doctrine of demons is a teaching inspired by demons that if believed and acted on will hinder someone from receiving salvation or will cause someone to fall away from salvation.

> *¹Now the Spirit expressly says that in latter times some will depart from the faith, giving heed to deceiving spirits and doctrines of demons, ²speaking lies in hypocrisy, having their own conscience seared with a hot iron, ³forbidding to marry… (1 Tim. 4:1–3)*

III.   TWO STAGES IN SATAN'S END-TIME PLAN

A.   There are two stages in Satan's end-time plan to be worshipped by all nations. Satan knows that it is a step too large for a compromising Christian, Muslim, Hindu, etc. suddenly to become a devoted Satan worshipper. Thus he will first call all to join a one-world religion of tolerance that will declare that all paths lead to God and salvation. As multitudes from various religious backgrounds are seduced into joining the harlot Babylon religion, it will weaken and defile their conscience concerning their religious heritage. Then Satan will demand that they worship him.

> *⁴They worshiped the dragon [Satan]…⁸All who dwell on the earth will worship him [Antichrist], whose names have not been written in the Book of Life of the Lamb slain from the foundation of the world. (Rev. 13:8)*

B.   People will break away from their religious heritage by renouncing their former beliefs. Once they leave their religious ideals, whether Christianity, Islam, Hinduism, or Buddhism, there will be no absolutes to keep them from worshipping Satan who appears as an angel of light (2 Cor. 11:14).

C.   The *voluntary* harlot Babylon religion will be replaced by a *mandatory* Antichrist religion.

    1.   First, people voluntarily join the harlot Babylon one-world religion of tolerance (Rev. 17).

    2.   Second, they will be forced to be Satan worshippers in the Antichrist religion (Rev. 13:4, 15).

D.   I agree with a popular view that sees Revelation 17–18 describing the fall of Babylon in two stages.

    1.   The first phase of the fall of Babylon (Rev. 17) relates to worldwide religious system of toleration and syncretism. The fall occurs at the beginning of the Great Tribulation at the hands of the ten kings (Rev. 17:16) who will burn it and replace it with Antichrist worship.

    2.   The second phase of her fall will be at the end of the Great Tribulation. It will focus on the collapse of the Antichrist's global economic system at God's hands (Rev. 18:8).

IV. THE GREAT HARLOT: HER SEDUCTIONS AND PERSECUTIONS (REV. 17:1–6)

A. Before the angel showed John the wealth and counterfeit beauty of the harlot religion, he showed him her inevitable judgment and sure defeat (Rev. 17:1). It will fail and be totally destroyed.

¹"…Come, I will show you the <u>judgment of the great harlot</u> who sits on many waters, ²with whom the <u>kings</u> of the earth <u>committed fornication</u>, and the <u>inhabitants</u> of the earth were made <u>drunk</u> with the wine of her fornication." ³…I saw a woman sitting on a scarlet beast [Antichrist]…⁴The woman was <u>arrayed in purple</u> and scarlet, and <u>adorned with gold</u>…having in her hand a <u>golden cup full of abominations</u> and the filthiness of her fornication. ⁵And on her forehead a name was written: MYSTERY, BABYLON THE GREAT, THE MOTHER OF HARLOTS AND OF THE ABOMINATIONS OF THE EARTH. ⁶I saw the woman, <u>drunk with the blood of the saints</u>…¹⁵He said to me, "The waters which you saw, where the harlot sits, are peoples, multitudes, nations, and tongues." (Rev. 17:1–6, 15)

B. ***Sits on many waters***: The harlot will sit on many nations (17:1, 15) or will have authority over the nations by seducing and controlling the world's most powerful leaders—the kings and merchants.

C. ***The kings***: The primary political leaders in the earth will understand some of the lies that empower the harlot system. However, they will support her agenda to gain her wealth, knowingly prostituting themselves or committing fornication with her in supporting her lies for money.

²"…with whom the <u>kings</u> of the earth <u>committed fornication</u>, and the <u>inhabitants</u> of the earth were made <u>drunk</u> with the wine of her fornication." (Rev. 17:2)

D. ***Made drunk***: The harlot's system will cause the nations to be drunk or intoxicated with her seductions that promise great benefits including humanitarian aid and a prosperous world economy. The nations will be overjoyed with her promises of prosperity and theology of tolerance. She will be a religion of affirmation and toleration without absolutes, with a counterfeit justice movement.

E. ***Sitting on the Beast***: The harlot will *sit on* or depend on the Antichrist who will *carry* her or will provide significant resource, validation, and protection for her.

³I saw a woman <u>sitting</u> on a scarlet beast [Antichrist] which was full of names of blasphemy…⁷"I will tell you the mystery of the woman and of the beast that <u>carries</u> her…" (Rev. 17:3, 7)

F. ***Arrayed in purple***: To be arrayed in purple speaks of her royal status or prominence. The harlot religion will have great prominence and will be embraced by the elite financial leaders of the earth.

⁴The woman was <u>arrayed</u> in purple [royalty] and scarlet, and <u>adorned</u> with gold…having in her hand a <u>golden cup</u> full of abominations and the filthiness of her fornication. (Rev. 17:4)

G. ***Adorned with gold***: It will be the wealthiest religious network in all of history.

H. ***A golden cup***: The harlot will have a golden cup from which she "serves" the nations. She will provide unprecedented humanitarian service, and her service will appear golden—valuable and good. It will facilitate unity in many nations. War will disappear for the first time in modern history, resulting in a temporary world peace. Paul prophesied that just before sudden destruction (Great Tribulation) comes, "they" or the nations shall proclaim peace and safety. (1 Thes. 5:3).

³…when they say, "<u>Peace and safety!</u>" then sudden destruction comes upon them… (1 Thes. 5:3)

I. *Full of abomination and filth*: She will offer a cup, or service, that is full of abomination and filth. Abomination refers to being associated with demonic activity since abominations in the Old Testament often referred to idolatrous or demonic activity. Filthiness points to its moral perversions.

J. The harlot will deceive the nations by sorcery, which is a combination of drugs and demonic power (witchcraft). Her dark, supernatural power will fascinate people, while appearing to be good. In my opinion, her worship music will be powerful, having a supernatural, demonic element to it.

23"…for by your [Babylon's] sorcery all the nations were deceived." (Rev. 18:23)

K. The harlot Babylon system is the context in which the nations will reach fullness in sin (Dan. 8:23). Then a king—the Antichrist—will appear on the world stage.

23"In the latter time of their kingdom, when the transgressors have reached their fullness, a king [Antichrist] shall arise…who understands sinister schemes." (Dan. 8:23)

L. The church across all the nations will expose the harlot for who she is. Then they will be hated by all nations for this. They will declare the seductive nature of her perversion and her judgment.

9"Then they will deliver you up to tribulation and kill you, and you will be hated by all nations for My name's sake. 10And then many will be offended, will betray one another, and will hate one another. 11Then many false prophets will rise up and deceive many." (Mt. 24:9–11)

M. Surprisingly, the harlot religion will be hated and destroyed by the jealousy of the ten kings who serve closest to the Antichrist (Dan. 7:7, 20, 24; Rev. 17:16). They will burn the harlot at the beginning of the Great Tribulation. Satan's kingdom is filled with hatred, not unity. Even when the harlot is at the height of her prominence, the Church will prophesy that she will be burned by the Antichrist's ten kings.

12"The ten horns which you saw are ten kings…16And the ten horns…on the beast [Antichrist], these will hate the harlot, make her desolate…and burn her with fire." (Rev. 17:12, 16)

N. In the middle of the final seven years of this age, I believe that the harlot religion of tolerance will be replaced with Antichrist worship. The Antichrist religion will be strict and without toleration. All who refuse to worship the Antichrist will be killed (Rev. 13:4–18). Satan's purpose for the harlot religion is to be the "forerunner" to prepare the nations for Antichrist worship.

V. THE HARLOT'S ORIGIN: THE TOWER OF BABEL

A. The harlot's name was a mystery to John. An angel gave him new information that had not yet been clearly revealed in Scripture—namely that the harlot is named Babylon the Great.

5And on her forehead a name was written: MYSTERY, BABYLON THE GREAT, THE MOTHER OF HARLOTS AND OF THE ABOMINATIONS OF THE EARTH. 6I saw the woman, drunk with the blood of the saints and with the blood of the martyrs of Jesus. (Rev. 17:5–6)

B. *The mother*: The harlot will be the mother of harlots or the source of false religion through history as well as the mother or source of abominations in the end times. Her offspring of false religion through history will crescendo and set the stage for the Antichrist in the end times.

C. **Drunk with blood**: The harlot will have a murderous heart despite her humanitarian appearance. The influence of the harlot will cause multitudes to be drunk or intoxicated with the blood of the saints who expose her. The more she kills, the bolder she will become in killing the saints.

D. **Babylon the great**: The angel revealed the harlot's name as Babylon. In other words, her origin was in Babylon—at the tower of Babel. By understanding what happened at the tower of Babel we gain insight into how she will operate. Babel was the first city to organize a rebellion against God.

VI. THE TOWER OF BABEL

A. The residents of Babel sought to build a tower whose "top is in the heavens." This refers to reaching into the spirit realm. It is not a reference to the height of a building that was made of mud bricks. The Lord had told the people to multiply and *fill the earth* (Gen. 1:28). The people of Babel wanted to *stay in* Babel to accomplish more together instead of going forth to fill the earth (Gen. 11:4).

⁴They said, "Come, let us build ourselves a city, and a tower whose <u>top is in the heavens</u>; let us <u>make a name for ourselves</u>, lest we be <u>scattered</u> abroad over the face of the whole earth." *(Gen. 11:4)*

B. Nothing they set their heart to do together would be withheld from them in terms of reaching their full potential in sin. The NASB/NIV translates this as nothing that they plan to do *"will be impossible for them."* This refers to their *unity in sin* to reach into the demonic realm (top in the heavens). The Lord was not referring to their architectural abilities having no limit, but to their progression in evil.

⁶The LORD said, "Indeed the people are one and they all have one language, and this is what they begin to do; <u>now nothing that they propose to do will be withheld from them</u>." *(Gen. 11:6)*

C. The Lord scattered their language to slow down their escalation of sin until the end times.

⁹Therefore its name is called <u>Babel</u>, because there the LORD <u>confused the language</u> of all the earth; and from there the LORD <u>scattered them abroad</u> over the face of all the earth. *(Gen. 11:9)*

D. In Jacob's dream he saw a ladder that gave him access to the heavenly realm in the will of God. Jesus referred to this reality as an "open heaven" where angels interact much with the earthly realm.

¹²He [Jacob] dreamed, and behold, a <u>ladder</u> was set up on the earth, and its <u>top reached to heaven</u>; and there the angels of God were ascending and descending on it. *(Gen. 28:12)*

⁵¹And He [Jesus] said to him, "Most assuredly, I say to you, hereafter you shall see <u>heaven open</u>, and the angels of God ascending and descending upon the Son of Man." *(Jn. 1:51)*

E. The harlot will have a "ladder of access" to the demonic realm enabling them to go to new heights of sin being assisted by demons. Those in Babel were seeking to reach a "demonic open heaven." In the Babylonian language, Babel means the *"gate of heaven,"* yet in Hebrew it means *"confusion."*

F. Billions of demons will be dislodged from their place in the heavens and cast to earth. I believe that in the end times there will be an unprecedented interaction between the demonic and human realm.

---

⁷And <u>war</u> broke out in heaven: Michael and his angels fought with the dragon…⁸but they did not prevail, nor was a place found for them in heaven any longer. ⁹So the great dragon [Satan] was <u>cast out</u>…he was cast to the earth, and <u>his angels [demons] were cast out with him</u>. (Rev 12:7–9)

G.   The time before Jesus' second coming is compared to the days of Noah in Genesis 6.

³⁷"But as the days of Noah were, so also will the coming of the Son of Man be." (Mt. 24:37)

H.   The people in Genesis 6 seemed to have walked in a sort of "counterfeit" open heaven as demons interacted with humans in an intense way (Gen. 6:4; 2 Pet. 2:4; Jude 6). There seems to have been a deep connection between the natural and demonic realm, resulting in violence (Gen. 6:7; 7:1–24).

⁵The LORD saw that the <u>wickedness of man was great</u> in the earth, and that every intent of the thoughts of his heart was <u>only evil continually</u>… ¹¹The earth was <u>filled with violence</u>. ¹²So God looked upon the earth, and indeed it was corrupt; for <u>all flesh had corrupted their way</u> on the earth. ¹³And God said to Noah, "The end of all flesh has come before Me, for the earth is <u>filled with violence</u> through them; and behold, I will <u>destroy</u> them with the earth." (Gen. 6:5–13)

VII.   THE END-TIME CONFLICT OVER THE TRUTH OF WHO JESUS IS

A.   In the end time there will be a battle for the truth about Jesus. Some believers will give heed to doctrines that lie about Jesus. The conflict will center on defining who Jesus is and how we love Him. We must love God on His terms—expressed with allegiance to the Jesus of the Bible.

B.   Tolerance that undermines God's Word is one of the primary characteristics in the social and religious movements that will prepare the way for the harlot Babylon.

C.   The body of Christ is to greatly value people with different beliefs and values. All humans possess great dignity and value in God's eyes. The body of Christ must not be willing to let them perish in hell by refusing to tell them the truth about Jesus and His salvation and love. The Church must lovingly and tenderly share the truth even as they serve and honor those who are resisting it.

D.   Three truths that offend those with a humanistic mindset:

1.   The deity of Jesus and His right to establish absolute standards and the definitions of love and morality for which the nations are accountable to Him.

2.   The only way of salvation is through Jesus.

3.   Jesus possesses the wisdom and love to judge sin both in time and eternity.

E.   Many today are resisting primary truths in the Scripture about Jesus and His salvation. We must not be intimidated by them, regardless of if they are famous people who work in the White House, host popular talk shows, fill stadiums with concerts for the poor, or lead mega-churches.

F.   The end-time Church will steward the greatest hope and justice movement in history. It will have a far superior hope than humanistic movements. Faithful witnesses of the truth about Jesus are the greatest hope-bringers in history. They will magnify Jesus' love, wisdom, and tenderness.

Session 12: Victory and the Restoration of All Things (Rev. 19–22)

I. JESUS' TRIUMPHAL ENTRY INTO JERUSALEM (REV. 19:11–21:8)

A. The fifth chronological section in Revelation describes Jesus' triumphal entry into Jerusalem to kill the Antichrist and all the kings of the earth (Rev. 19:11–21) and establish His throne in Jerusalem. Next, Satan will be cast into prison (Rev. 20:1–3). Then Jesus will put the saints on thrones for 1,000 years (Rev. 20:4–6). After 1,000 years, Satan will be released from prison to test the nations, and then the rebels will be judged with Satan (Rev. 20:7–10). Next, the great white throne judgment of unbelievers will occur (Rev. 20:11–15). After that the Lord will establish the new heaven and earth (Rev 21:1–8), and the Father's throne will come to earth (Rev 21:3).

B. John described seven scenes in Revelation 19:11–21:
Scene 1: Twelve aspects of Jesus' triumphal entry into Jerusalem are highlighted (19:11–16).
Scene 2: Jesus will defeat the Antichrist at the Battle of Jerusalem (19:17–21).
Scene 3: Satan will be cast into prison for 1,000 years (20:1–3).
Scene 4: Saints will be given the governmental leadership over the earth (20:4–6).
Scene 5: Satan is released after 1,000 years, giving all a choice to obey or not (20:7–10).
Scene 6: God's great white throne judgment of all His enemies (20:11–15).
Scene 7: The Father will establish His throne with His people on the new earth (21:1–8).

C. Revelation 19 gives us more detail about the beauty of Jesus as a Bridegroom, King, and Judge than any other passage. Each phrase is significant—they are "hints" that we are to search out by using the Bible to get a greater picture of what the Spirit is saying here about Jesus' beauty.

II. THE BATTLE FOR JERUSALEM

A. ***The battle of Jerusalem***: All the nations will gather against Jerusalem (Joel 3:2, 12; Zech. 12:3; 14:2; Zeph. 3:8; cf. Ezek. 38:4; 39:2; Rev. 16:14). God's end-time plan is "Jerusalem-centric."

³"In that day that I will make __Jerusalem__ a very heavy stone…all who would heave it away will surely be cut in pieces, though __all nations of the earth__ are gathered against it." (Zech. 12:3)

B. The battle for Jerusalem is the spiritual, political, and military struggle for the control of Jerusalem. This is one of the most significant battlefronts in the spirit today and will be won only by Jesus' second coming to end the Armageddon campaign. The valley of Megiddo, in the northern part of Israel, will function as the military staging area where the kings of the earth and their armies gather.

C. John described Jesus' great victory at the Battle of Jerusalem of which the OT prophets foretold. Jesus will enter Jerusalem, arriving at the perfect time to rescue the remnant of Israel (Zech. 14:5).

²I will gather __all the nations to battle against Jerusalem__; the city shall be taken…³Then the LORD will go forth [Jesus' second coming] __and fight against those nations__…⁴His feet will stand on the Mount of Olives…and the Mount of Olives shall be split in two…making a very large valley… ⁵Then __you shall flee__ through My mountain valley…Yes, you shall flee…the LORD my God will come, and all the saints with You. (Zech. 14:2–5)

III.   THE BEAUTY OF JESUS WILL BE OPENLY SEEN

A.   In Revelation 19, we see Jesus' beauty; we see how far Jesus is willing to go for the sake of love and how committed He is to justice. In this context, the beauty of the Lord will be revealed. As we meditate on what He will do at that time, we are able to see His personality behind the events.

²In that day the Branch of the LORD [Jesus] shall be <u>beautiful and glorious</u>. (Isa. 4:2)

¹⁷Your eyes will see the King in <u>His beauty</u>… (Isa. 33:17)

B.   *Summary*: The most dramatic events in world history will occur in context to the greatest military campaign that will be undergirded by the greatest prayer movement contending against the greatest oppression to see the greatest justice movement fulfilled across the whole earth.

IV.   JESUS' TRIUMPHAL ENTRY (REV. 19:11–21)

A.   Isaiah described Jesus entering the battle scene just outside Jerusalem as He marches to Jerusalem from Edom—modern-day Jordan (Isa. 62:1–63:6). He described Jesus as trampling the nations as one treads grapes in a winepress (Isa. 63:3; Joel 3:13; Rev. 14:20; 19:15).

¹Who is this who comes from <u>Edom</u> [Jordan]…this One [Jesus] who is glorious…<u>traveling</u> in the greatness of His strength?…²Why is Your apparel red, and Your garments like one who <u>treads in the winepress</u>? ³"I have trodden the winepress…and <u>trampled</u> them in My fury; <u>their blood</u> is sprinkled upon <u>My garments</u>, and I have <u>stained all My robes</u>." (Isa. 63:1–3)

B.   John saw Jesus traveling to Jerusalem for the final battle in natural history (Rev. 19:19–21).

¹¹I saw heaven opened, and behold, a white horse. And He who sat on him was called <u>Faithful</u> and <u>True</u>, and in righteousness He judges and <u>makes war</u>. ¹²His eyes were like a flame of fire, and on His head were <u>many crowns</u>…¹³He was clothed with a robe <u>dipped in blood</u>…¹⁴The armies in heaven…followed Him on white horses. ¹⁵Now out of His mouth goes a sharp sword, that with it He should <u>strike the nations</u>…He Himself treads the winepress of the…wrath of Almighty God. ¹⁶And He has on His robe…a name written: KING OF KINGS AND LORD OF LORDS. (Rev. 19:11–16)

C.   John saw Jesus as the faithful and true warrior who makes war with the Antichrist (Rev. 19:11).

1.   *White horse*: Jesus will make His triumphal entry into Jerusalem on a white horse, as the conquering King in the context of a military conflict. White speaks of victory and purity. There are real horses in the heavenly realm. Elijah, Elisha, and Zechariah saw horses with heavenly chariots (2 Kgs. 2:11; 6:17; Zech. 6:1–5). The saints will ride horses (v. 14).

2.   *He judges*: Jesus will intervene with judgment in order to put things right. His judgments include establishing new leaders, laws, and policies that will help the poor (Isa. 11:4).

⁴With righteousness He shall <u>judge the poor</u>…He shall strike the earth… (Isa. 11:4)

3. ***He makes war***: The most extreme judgment in history will occur in the largest, most violent battle of history. Jesus will restore order by destroying wicked governments on the earth. The *"Jesus of Christmas"* will bring peace and goodwill to men (Lk. 2:14) by waging a just war against evil as the *"Jesus of Armageddon."* He will use war to establish peace and justice. The Antichrist starts this war (Rev. 11:7; 12:7, 17; 13:4, 7; 17:14; 19:19; cf. Dan. 7:21; 9:26).

4. ***Faithful and true***: Jesus is faithful to fulfill His promises and true to His loving nature in all that He does. Even in battle, Jesus is faithful to love and justice, doing all according to truth.

D. John saw Jesus' eyes, His many crowns, and His mysterious name (Rev. 19:12).

[12]His <u>eyes were like a flame of fire</u>, and on His head were <u>many crowns</u>. (Rev. 19:12)

1. ***Eyes of fire***: Jesus' eyes speak of His zealous love and perfect knowledge. Eyes of fire speak of His burning heart of desire for His people.

2. ***Many crowns***: Jesus' crowns speak of His past and future victories.

E. Jesus' robe will be stained with the blood of His enemies as He fulfills God's Word (Rev. 19:13).

[13]He was clothed with a <u>robe dipped in blood</u>, and His name is called The <u>Word of God</u>. (19:13)

1. ***Robe dipped in blood***: His robe (long outer garment) will be splattered with the blood of His enemies. Most scholars see this as referring to the blood of Jesus' enemies being on His robe. The word *dipped* comes from the Greek word *baptô*, from which we get *baptize* which some translate as "sprinkled" or "soaked" in blood. His robes will be stained with blood from the battle in His march to Jerusalem from Edom (Isa. 63:3).

   [3]"Their blood is sprinkled upon My garments, and I have <u>stained all My robes</u>." (Isa. 63:3)

   a. The blood on His clothing denotes His intimate involvement in the war. Jesus will be up close and personal in the battle. It is a statement that He believes in this war. He will not be ashamed of shedding blood in the process of delivering the nations from such evil.

2. ***Word of God***: All that Jesus does in the battle of Jerusalem is true to Scripture. His goals, motives, and attitudes in this great battle will be totally consistent with Scripture. His name— "The Word of God"—emphasizes His promise to fill the earth with justice through this battle.

F. Jesus desires partnership with His people, even as He takes over the nations (Rev. 19:14).

[14]The <u>armies</u> in heaven, clothed in fine linen, white and clean, <u>followed Him</u> on white horses. (Rev. 19:14)

[24]"Father, <u>I desire</u> that they also whom You gave Me <u>may be with Me where I am</u>, that they may behold My glory which You have given Me…" (Jn. 17:24)

G. *Armies followed Him*: In my opinion, these armies refer to the saints (1 Thes. 4:14; cf. Zech. 14:5).

H. ***White and clean***: The armies of heaven will be dressed in *fine linen*, *white* and *clean* (Rev. 19:14). This clothing is similar to the saints in their bridal attire as seen in Revelation 19:7–8.

I.   Jesus' actions in judging the nations include striking them with the sword of His mouth, ruling them with a rod of iron, and treading the winepress of God's wrath (Rev. 19:15). His end-time judgments will be released by the decree of His mouth (Isa. 11:4).

> *15Out of His mouth goes a sharp sword, that with it He should <u>strike the nations</u>. And He Himself will rule them with a <u>rod of iron</u>. He Himself <u>treads the winepress</u> of…wrath… (Rev. 19:15)*

J.   *King of kings*: All the nations on earth will see Jesus as the King of kings (Rev. 19:16). He will take over everything forever, for the glory of God and the good of His people.

> *16He has on His robe and on His thigh a <u>name</u> written: <u>KING OF KINGS</u>… (Rev. 19:16)*

V.   THE SPIRIT HIGHLIGHTS FOUR ASPECTS OF JESUS' ACTIVITY (REV. 19:17–21)

A.   Jesus will gather the birds for a great supper, feasting on the Antichrist's army (Rev. 19:17–18). Jesus has power over all creation, even the birds. There will be a supernatural gathering of birds that will clean up the carnage of the dead armies (to prevent disease at the start of the Millennium?).

> *17I saw an angel…saying to <u>all the birds</u> that fly in the midst of heaven, "Come and gather together for the <u>supper of the great God</u>, 18that you may <u>eat the flesh of kings</u>, the flesh of captains, the flesh of mighty men, the flesh of horses…and the <u>flesh of all people</u>…" (Rev. 19:17–18)*

B.   All kings will be gathered with their armies (Rev. 19:19; cf. Joel 3:2, 12; Zech. 14:2; Zeph. 3:8). This shows the global scope of the hostility and why Jesus' violent action is necessary.

> *19And I saw the beast [Antichrist], the <u>kings of the earth</u>, and <u>their armies</u>, gathered together to make <u>war against Him</u> [Jesus] who sat on the horse and against <u>His army</u>. (Rev. 19:19)*

C.   The Antichrist will be defeated in the sight of all the nations (Rev. 19:20).

> *20Then the beast [Antichrist] was <u>captured</u>, and with him the false prophet… (Rev. 19:20)*

D.   Jesus attends to every detail, even the cleanup of the dead (Rev. 19:21). All the kings and their armies will be killed (Ps. 110:5–6; Isa. 24:6, 21–21; 66:24). It will take seven months to bury the bones of the dead (Ezek. 39:11–16) and seven years to burn the weapons (Ezek. 39:9).

> *21And the <u>rest were killed</u> with the sword which proceeded from the mouth of Him who sat on the horse. And <u>all the birds</u> were filled with their flesh. (Rev. 19:21)*

E.   The pinnacle of the second-coming, royal procession will be Jesus' reentry into Jerusalem to be officially received by the governmental leaders of Israel as their Messianic King.

> *39"I say to you [governmental leaders in Jerusalem], you shall see Me no more till you say, 'Blessed is He who comes in the name of the LORD!'" (Mt. 23:39)*

F.   Jesus will be celebrated as the Son of David in a hosanna coronation parade hosted by the leaders of Israel. They will open the gates of Jerusalem to Jesus in an official declaration of Him as their King after He rescues them to end the Armageddon campaign.

> *7Lift up your heads, O you <u>gates</u> [of Jerusalem]! And be lifted up, you everlasting doors! And the King of glory shall come in. 8<u>Who is this King of glory</u>? The LORD strong and mighty, the LORD <u>mighty in battle</u> [Armageddon campaign]. (Ps. 24:7–8)*

VI. THE MILLENNIAL KINGDOM AND THE FINAL JUDGMENT (REV. 20:1–15)

A. Satan will be bound with supernatural chains and then cast into the pit or prison (Rev. 20:1–3).

> *²He [an angel] <u>laid hold</u> of the dragon, that serpent of old…the Devil and Satan, and <u>bound</u> him for a thousand years; ³and he <u>cast</u> him into the bottomless pit, and <u>shut him up</u>, and set a <u>seal</u> on him, so that he should deceive the nations no more…after these things he must be released for a little while. (Rev. 20:2–3)*

B. The saints will be given governmental leadership of the earth for one thousand years (Rev. 20:4–6).

> *⁴I saw thrones, and <u>they sat on them</u>, and <u>judgment was committed to them</u>. Then I saw the souls of those who had been beheaded for their witness to Jesus…and <u>they lived</u> and <u>reigned with Christ for a thousand years</u>…⁶Blessed and holy is he who has part in the first resurrection…they shall be <u>priests</u> of God and of Christ, and shall <u>reign</u> with Him 1,000 years. (Rev. 20:4–6)*

  1. At this time the kingdom of God will be openly manifested worldwide, affecting every sphere of life. The result will be a 1,000-year period of unprecedented blessing for the earth as Jesus establishes righteousness and prosperity, restoring the agriculture, atmosphere, and animal life to some of the conditions that were seen in the Garden of Eden (Rev. 20:1–6; cf. Isa. 2:1–4; 9:6–9; 11:1–16; 51:1–8; 60–62; 65:17–25; Ps. 2:6–12; 110:1–7; Deut. 8; 28; Mt. 5:5; 6:10; 17:11; 19:28; 28:19; Acts 1:6; 3:21).

  2. In the Millennium all the kings of the earth will be saved and worship Jesus (Ps. 72:11; 102:15; 138:4; 148:11; Isa. 62:2; Rev. 21:24).

  3. ***They sat on them***: The saints of verses 14 and 19 are the subject of "they sat" (20:4). Jesus will govern the earth in partnership with resurrected saints (Rev. 2:26–27; 3:21; 5:10; 22:5; cf. Mt. 19:28; 25:23; Lk. 19:17–19; 22:29–30; Rom 8:17; 1 Cor. 6:2–3; 2 Tim. 2:12).

C. The Lord will allow Satan, the "snake" of Genesis 3, back into the garden to offer the human race independence from God in order to reveal their hearts. This will show God's justice in judgment.

> *⁷Now when the thousand years have expired, Satan will be <u>released from his prison</u> ⁸and will go out to <u>deceive the nations</u>…⁹They…surrounded the camp of the saints and the beloved city. And fire came down from God out of heaven and devoured them. ¹⁰The devil…was cast into the lake of fire and brimstone where the beast and the false prophet are. And they will be tormented day and night forever and ever. (Rev. 20:7–10)*

D. God will openly manifest the truth about the *depth of human sin* and about Satan as being *incurably evil*. Satan will not be rehabilitated. God will demonstrate the justice of His eternal judgments by showing that rehabilitation will not occur and that men rebel even in an ideal environment because they love sin. Men will not be able to blame their sin on their difficult circumstances.

E. The great white throne is God's final judgment of all His enemies (Rev. 20:11–15).

> *¹¹Then I saw a great white throne…¹²And I saw the dead, small and great, standing before God, and books were opened. And another book was opened, which is the Book of Life. And the dead were judged according to their works, by the things which were written in the books…¹⁴Then Death and Hades were cast into the lake of fire. This is the second death. ¹⁵And anyone not found written in the Book of Life was cast into the lake of fire. (Rev. 20:11–15)*

VII. THE FATHER ESTABLISHES HIS THRONE ON EARTH (REV. 21:1–8)

A.   The high point of history is the Father dwelling on earth with humans (Rev. 21:3). God's purpose has always been to live together with His people *face to face on this earth*. The Father's throne permanently coming to earth is the ultimate reality that God accomplished through Christ.

> *[1]I saw a <u>new heaven</u> and a <u>new earth</u>, for the first heaven and the first earth had <u>passed away</u>. Also there was no more sea. [2]Then I, John, saw the holy city, <u>New Jerusalem</u>, coming down out of heaven from God, prepared as a bride adorned for her husband. [3]And I heard a loud voice from heaven saying, "<u>Behold, the tabernacle of God is with men, and He will dwell with them,</u> and they shall be His people. God Himself will be with them and be their God."(Rev. 21:1–3)*

B.   The new earth is the permanent resting place of the New Jerusalem. Some debate whether this present earth will be *renovated* or *annihilated* after the Millennium and a new earth created. The earth will continue forever (Ps. 37:29; 78:69; 104:5; 105:10–11; 125:1–2; cf. 1 Chr. 23:25; 28:8; Isa. 60:21; Ezek. 37:25; Joel 3:20). The words "passed away" in (v. 1) are the same as in 2 Cor. 5:17.

VIII. NEW JERUSALEM: THE RESTORATION OF ALL THINGS (REV. 21–22)

A.   Revelation 21–22 is an angelic explanation that follows the glory and judgment described in the Revelation 19–20. Jesus will restore to us all that He intended in creating the Garden of Eden.

> *[19]"Repent…that your sins may be blotted out, so that…[20] He [the Father] may send Jesus… [21]whom heaven must receive [keep] <u>until the times of restoration of all things</u>, which God has spoken by the mouth of all His holy prophets since the world began." (Acts 3:19–21)*

B.   The description of the City as the *Holy of Holies*—an external view (21:9–21)

     1.   *The City's design*: a cube (21:16) like the Holy of Holies in Solomon's temple.
     2.   *The City's adornment*: It has eight of the precious stones (21:19–20) that the high priest wore on his breastplate when entering the Holy of Holies, signifying nearness to God (Ex. 28:17–20; 39:10).
     3.   *The City's glory*: It is filled with the *shekinah* glory as in the temple (2 Chr. 5–7), yet with the brightness of ancient jasper that is different from modern jasper (Rev. 21:11, 23; 22:5).
     4.   *The City's construction*: gates (21:12b–14), walls (21:12a, 14–18), foundations (21:12, 19–20), and streets (21:21; 22:2).
     5.   *The City's size*: The walls are 1,380 miles in length, height, and width (Rev. 21:12b–14).

C.   The description of the City as the *Garden of Eden*—an internal view (21:22–22:5). He described the City's beauty (21:22–27) and its life with face-to-face communion with God (22:1–5).

D.   It is a worshipping City with no temple (21:22; 22:4a); an illuminated City with no sun (21:23; 22:5); a governmental City with God's Throne (21:24, 26; 22:3–5d); a servant City that works (21:25b; 22:3c, 5a), and a holy City without any sin (21:27, 8; 22:14–15).

International House *of* Prayer

MISSIONS BASE OF KANSAS CITY

....

24/7 Live Worship with Prayer since 1999

On September 19, 1999, a prayer meeting began that continues to this day; from dawn to dusk and through the watches of the night, by the grace of God, prayer and worship have continued twenty-four hours a day, seven days a week.

Learn more at ihopkc.org/about

THE PRAYER ROOM EXPERIENCE

Unceasing is a monthly subscription to our exclusive, growing library of spontaneous worship recorded live at the International House of Prayer. Every month we add our best songs, prophetic moments, intercession cycles, and instrumental selahs.

Learn more at unceasingworship.com

International House of Prayer Missions Base, 3535 E. Red Bridge Road, Kansas City, MO 64137
(816) 763-0200 | info@ihopkc.org

INTERNATIONAL HOUSE *of* PRAYER UNIVERSITY

MINISTRY · MUSIC · MEDIA · MISSIONS

· ·

ENCOUNTER GOD. DO HIS WORKS. CHANGE THE WORLD.

ihopkc.org/ihopu

· ·

International House of Prayer University (IHOPU) is a full-time Bible school which exists to equip this generation in the Word and in the power of the Holy Spirit for the bold proclamation of the Lord Jesus and His return.

As part of the International House of Prayer, our Bible school is built around the centrality of the Word and 24/7 prayer with worship, equipping students in the Word and the power of the Spirit for the bold proclamation of the Lord Jesus and His kingdom. Training at IHOPU forms not only minds but also lifestyle and character, to sustain students for a life of obedience, humility, and anointed service in the kingdom. Our curriculum combines in-depth biblical training with discipleship, practical service, outreach, and works of compassion.

IHOPU is for students who long to encounter Jesus. With schools of ministry, music, media, and missions, our one- to four-year certificate and diploma programs prepare students to engage in the Great Commission and obey Jesus' commandments to love God and people.

> "What Bible School has 'prayer' on its curriculum? The most important thing a man can study is the prayer part of the Book. But where is this taught?
>
> Let us strip off the last bandage and declare that many of our presidents and teachers do not pray, shed no tears, know no travail. Can they teach what they do not know?"
>
> –Leonard Ravenhill, *Why Revival Tarries*

International House *of* Prayer

INTERNSHIPS

INTRO TO IHOPKC • FIRE IN THE NIGHT • ONE THING INTERNSHIP
SIMEON COMPANY • HOPE CITY INTERNSHIP

ihopkc.org/internships

Internships exist to see people equipped with the Word of God, ministering in the power of the Holy Spirit, engaged in intercession, and committed to outreach and service.

Our five internships are three to six months long and accommodate all seasons of life. The purpose of the internships is to further prepare individuals of all ages as intercessors, worshipers, messengers, singers, and musicians for the work of the kingdom. While each internship has a distinctive age limit, length, and schedule, they all share the same central training components: corporate prayer and worship meetings, classroom instruction, practical ministry experience, outreach, and relationship-building.

Biblical teaching in all of the internships focuses on intimacy with Jesus, ministry in the power of the Holy Spirit, the forerunner ministry, evangelizing the lost, justice, and outreach. Interns also receive practical, hands-on training in the prophetic and healing ministries.

Upon successful completion of a six-month internship or two three-month tracks, some will stay and apply to join IHOPKC staff.

Our IHOPKC Leadership Team

Our leadership team of over a hundred and fifty men and women, with diversity of experience, background, and training, represent twenty countries and thirty denominations and oversee eighty-five departments on our missions base. With a breadth of experience in pastoral ministry, missions work, education, and the marketplace, this team's training in various disciplines includes over forty master's degrees and ten doctorates.

International House of Prayer Missions Base, 3535 E. Red Bridge Road, Kansas City, MO 64137
(816) 763-0200 | internships@ihopkc.org

MIKE BICKLE
TEACHING LIBRARY
—— *Free Teaching & Resource Library* ——

This International House of Prayer resource library, encompassing more than thirty years of Mike's teaching ministry, provides access to hundreds of resources in various formats, including streaming video, downloadable video, and audio, accompanied by study notes and transcripts, absolutely free of charge.

You will find some of Mike's most requested titles, including *The Gospel of Grace*; *The First Commandment*; *Jesus, Our Magnificent Obsession*; *Romans: Theology of Holy Passion*; *The Sermon on the Mount: The Kingdom Lifestyle*; and much more.

We encourage you to freely copy any of these teachings to share with others or use in any way: "our copyright is the right to copy." Older messages are being prepared and uploaded from Mike's teaching archives, and all new teachings are added immediately.

Visit mikebickle.org

International House of Prayer Missions Base, 3535 E. Red Bridge Road, Kansas City, MO 64137
(816) 763-0200 | info@ihopkc.org | ihopkc.org